WALPOLE'S QUEEN OF COMEDY

THE SECOND TIME.

At the Theatre-Royal in the Haymarket,

This prefent MONDAY, July 13, 1778,

Will be Prefented a NEW PIECE in FOUR ACTS, called

The SUICIDE,
A COMEDY!

THE PRINCIPAL PARTS BY

Mr. PALMER,

Mr. AICKIN,

Mr. EDWIN,

Mr. R. PALMER,

Mr. WEBB,

Mr. LAMASH, Mr. GARDNER,

Mr. BADDELEY,

Mr. BLISSETT,

Mr. MASSEY,

Mr. DAVIS, Mr. EGAN,

Mr. PEIRCE, Mr. STEVENS,

And Mr. BANNISTER.

Mrs. WEBB,

Miss HALE,

And Miss FARREN.

With a Prologue to be Spoken by Mr. PALMER,

And an Epilogue by Miss FARREN.

To which will be added, a DRAMATIC NOVEL, called

POLLY HONEYCOMBE.

Mr. Honeycombe, Mr. PARSONS,

Scribble, Mr. R. PALMER, Ledger, Mr. GARDNER,

Mrs. Honeycombe, Miss PLATT, Nurfe, Mrs. LOVE,

And Polly Honeycombe, Mrs. HITCHCOCK.

The Doors to be opened at Six o'Clock, and the Performance begin precifely at Seven.
Servants to keep Places are to be at the Door in SUFFOLK-STREET by Five o'Clock.

WALPOLE'S
QUEEN OF COMEDY

ELIZABETH FARREN
Countess of Derby

Suzanne Bloxam

First published in 1988 by
SUZANNE BLOXAM
1 Gothic Cottages, The Street, Great Chart,
Ashford, Kent TN23 3AW

© Suzanne Bloxam 1988

British Library Cataloguing in Publication Data

Bloxam, Suzanne, 1912 –
Walpole's Queen of Comedy: a biography of Elizabeth Farren,
Countess of Derby
1. Great Britain. Theatre. Acting. Farren, Elizabeth, Countess of
Derby, 1759 – 1829
I. Title
792'. 028' 0924

ISBN 1 - 85421 - 031 - 9

Designed and produced by the SPA Ltd,Upton-upon-Severn
Printed and bound in Great Britain by Billing & Sons Ltd, Worcester

Dedicated to Elizabeth Chomley Farran, 1878 – 1976, who treasured and guarded family portraits, miniatures, letters and notes of the eighteenth and nineteenth centuries.

Thanks are due to the following for permission to use material included in this book: Theatre Museum Covent Garden, Sotheby's, The Earl of Derby M.C., National Gallery of Victoria, Melbourne, Australia, Trustees of The British Museum, University of Bristol Theatre Collection, National Portrait Gallery, N.G.W. Bloxam, Christies

Author's Note

The two spellings of the surname FARRAN and FARREN in the same family in this narrative will cause surprise, but it is unavoidable. Spellings of surnames in the eighteenth century and earlier are well known to have been erratic but although Irish newspapers and magazines of the relevant period frequently use 'en' for members of the family, their own signatures never vary from 'an' – and the surname is always included, even from mother to daughter at the end of a letter. The same practice continues in the family today.

It might have been supposed that George Farran, Elizabeth's father, changed 'an' for 'en' when he took to the stage but the truth is that even when he formed his own company of players, he adhered to the correct spelling. [See *The Georgian Theatre in Wessex;* Arnold Hare.]

Further confusion is caused by Elizabeth's use of the suffix 'en' on the stage and the fact that she signed that way too except in the marriage register. Lord Derby's family was well aware of the correct spelling on this account as well as through correspondence wtih her Irish cousins.

No connection exists between the Farran family of Dublin and the Farren family of Cork. Neither is there any link between the Dublin family and that of the famous actor, contemporary with Elizabeth, William Farren who made his London debut within a few weeks of Elizabeth's first London appearance on 9th June, 1777.

It is probable that ignorance of the correct spelling allied to carelessness in using the more usual 'en' in England in the first place, led to common usage thereafter.

The MARRIAGE of CUPID & PSYCHE.

Contents

Foreword

The impetus for this biography of Elizabeth Farren, the eighteenth century actress, stemmed from the full length portrait of her by Sir Thomas Lawrence, P.R.A., which was exhibited in London in 1979. Sir Michael Levey, late Director of the National Gallery has very kindly written these words for inclusion here.

There was an opportunity in 1979 to see back in England, and in the context of other Lawrence portraits, the full length portrait of Elizabeth Farren which Lawrence painted in 1789 and exhibited at the Royal Academy the following year. The portrait went to America early in this century, became the property of the Metropolitan Museum, New York, in 1940 and had not been seen over here since its departure. It was included in the National Portrait Gallery's exhibition of Sir Thomas Lawrence's paintings and drawings, in the same room as the artist's full length of *Queen Charlotte*, also exhibited by him at the Royal Academy in 1790.

The portrait of Miss Farren was one of Lawrence's earliest public successes, and it is easy to see why. It remains among his finest work, though he was only twenty when he painted it and had an active career of forty years before him. The vivacity, elegance and charm of Miss Farren's appearance are captured by Lawrence's concept of showing her, as he wrote himself, "in private . . . unaided by professional character". She is shown in a wonderful *plein-air* setting of summer sky and landscape, with a hint of sea beyond the glistening meadows through which she steps in white satin, almost trailing her huge muff, adorned with a simple bow, poised like a blue velvet butterfly on soft-seeming fur. Lawrence's response extends beyond the sitter's face, to the various textures of her clothes, cape, furs and skin-tight leather glove, all conveyed through virtuoso handling of oil paint. The picture retains an almost startling freshness and at the National Portrait Gallery's exhibition confronted visitors with the challenging illusionism of Miss Farren pausing before them that must have been felt by contemporaries when they first saw it. It is very much the portrait not of an actress but of a sprightly, engaging personality, highly conscious of her own attraction and yet natural, as well as in a natural setting, and perhaps already on the way to considering retirement from the stage.

Prologue

On a platform, surrounded by merry people in the centre of the market square, the Mayor of Salisbury enjoyed a bout of single-stick with Frederick Fitzmontague, a member of Farran's Strolling Company. Frederick had gone ahead of the company to seek permission to set up a stage and perform in the market place.

Much to Fitzmontague's surprise, after obtaining the mayor's goodwill and setting up the platform, the chief magistrate made it clear that he was not only game but keen to try his skill at single-stick with the professional.

For a time all went well, burgesses and country bumpkins alike were enjoying the fun and the professional added to it by allowing his adversary to score a number of hits. However, he ended the fray by delivering an almighty stroke on the Mayor's skull, laying him out and causing him to become confused. The professional apologised profusely and the Mayor replied, 'Don't mention it, there's nothing in it,' but his politeness hid his wounded pride and he was really angry. All might yet have been well had the fuzzy-headed Mayor not heard the distant beating of a drum at that very moment coming from the Fisherton direction. Drums announcing itinerant players – or pompers as they were often called – were anathema to the Mayor of Salisbury and the sound brought him to his senses immediately.

The Farran Company drummer was short and sturdy with a big, red nose; he doubled being the drummer with being the comedian. He was followed by several couples of men and women, all light-hearted and happy. After them came a cart with stage properties and luggage and the rear of the procession was brought up by a fine gentleman leading a little girl by the hand. Something about them

11

placed them above those in front. In short, to use an Irishism, George Farran and Elizabeth were "a cut above the common".

The Mayor was in no state to look kindly on anyone; his head ached from the blow and the din of the drum. Not recalling he had already given his good-will for the performance – a fact of which George Farran was also oblivious – he vented his wrath on George, saying, 'Salisbury is a godly place. As a servant of the King I am bound to allow only respectable amusements.'

In vain did George point out that the King himself favoured the theatre. This was worse than any blow for the Mayor and the ensuing altercation led to a riot. George was arrested and sent to prison – mainly because the populace took his side in the argument.

By that time, it was dark and pouring with rain. The mob dispersed. Poor little Elizabeth's world had fallen about her ears with her beloved father in prison and her mother miles away in Liverpool. Weeping bitterly she was led to some lodgings by a kindly actress while Frederick Fitzmontague went to his lodgings on the opposite side of the square, over Mr Burroughs' upholsterer's shop.

After a miserable, sleepless night, Elizabeth was up soon after dawn to prepare a bowl of bread-and-milk for her father's breakfast and when it was ready, she opened the door and looked out; there had been a sharp frost and it was snowing. At the same time, Burroughs' young son was looking out on the opposite side and soon he saw a figure moving in the gloom; it was Elizabeth. He watched her moving slowly over the ice, looking like a nymph carrying an urn. Suddenly she stopped dead, aware and alarmed at the danger of her journey. Sizing up the situation the boy took a run and slid across the ice arriving at Elizabeth's side – though not before she cried out in fear of an approaching collision. She wouldn't let him carry her precious burden but accepted his supporting arm and they negotiated the perilous walk to the prison together.

George could see them coming and greeted Elizabeth, 'God bless you my own child.' She asked him whatever Mama and all their friends would say if they knew how they were spending Christmas morning. 'Things unknown are unfelt my darling,' replied George. 'We will tell them nothing until Fortune gilds over the memory.'

The window was too high for Elizabeth[1] to reach so young Burroughs lifted her up to the bars so that her father could take the bowl. Momentarily she became her merry self for the first time since the previous evening but her happiness was short-lived when she remembered their plight. At that very moment the town constable appeared, accompanied by a man with a clerical collar. He announced that the prisoner was to be set free due to the intervention of "the Reverend Snodgrass" recently arrived in Salisbury. Elizabeth clapped her hands for joy for Mr Snodgrass was one of her father's company! In the off season he was employed by a religious society, preaching sermons on the highways about the evils of the drama. This had earned him the nick-name of "Missionary Jack". On hearing of George's predicament, he had raided the props, donned his clerical collar and clothes and visited the Mayor in his Parlour. He asked to contribute to the Christmas festivities. 'Was there a prisoner perhaps whose freedom might be bought?' And the trick had worked.[2]

Later in the holiday season Elizabeth made her first stage appearance. She played Columbine in the Christmas pantomime. She showed the audience that despite her youth, she could act, she could dance and she could sing.

Prologue – Footnotes

1. In the National Portrait Gallery records there is a note of an imaginary watercolour of the scene at the prison window, which was painted by Thomas Roberts and shown at The Exhibition of English Watercolours in 1873. It was sold for £60 but its whereabouts are unknown. Beneath it the artist had written:

   Lizzie Farren (afterwards Countess of Derby) bringing her father's breakfast to the prison.

2. Doran, Dr John, F.S.A., Knights and Their Days. 1856 pp 336–339.

Chapter One

George Farran was born in Dublin circa 1731 of a Huguenot family which settled there prior to the Revocation of the Edict of Nantes in 1785. His father, John, was a wine merchant, a man of substance who owned lands at Strabane, leased lands at Trelick[1] and appears in the City of Dublin Freeman's Roll for 1718 as "John ffarran".

John's choice of school for his elder son George, has great relevance for this story for the founder of it was the Reverend Dr Thomas Sheridan, grandfather of the playwright, and he followed the English custom of insisting on drama in the school curriculum – the only Irish school to do so.

The school took place in his large family house in Capel Street and his close friend, Jonathan Swift, Dean of St Patrick's Cathedral, has left a vivid picture of the ramshackle interior in verse. He describes the steps as "torn to rags by boys and ball", the sitting-room door "besmear'd with chalk, and carv'd with knives" and the broken down chair which collapsed and let him down "upon his Reverend Deanship's bum."[2]

Plays by Shakespeare or classical authors were the rule at Capel Street and they were acted in the original Greek or Latin, often with Prologues and or Epilogues by Jonathan Swift in English. On occasions the Lord Lieutenant of Ireland and the Archbishop of Dublin with other people of consequence were in the audience and the performances became so popular that an outside hall had to be hired so that the competition began to alarm the public theatres.

By George's advent, Dr Sheridan had gone to a country living but his principal usher, the Reverend Moses Magill, ran the establishment on the same lines with continued emphasis on drama, and George, though only very young at the time, soon became passionately interested in plays and players. This greatly disturbed his father for at that time, acting was not considered a suitable profession for a gentleman's son. As soon as George was old enough to go away from home, he was sent as a boarder to Mr Shackleton's school in Ballitore, Co. Kildare. This was on 29th June 1744 when he was about 13.[3] Mr Shackleton was a Quaker and plays were anathema to him, so John Farran hoped his son's great interest in the theatre would die. In the event the move came too late.

After school, George's brother Curtis was sent to Trinity College, Dublin and became a scholar there; not so George. He had been indented to his father's wine business for five years but he broke the indenture and was apprenticed to a Surgeon-Apothecary in Cork. Why he was sent there is not known and remains a mystery. He had no relatives in the city and there is no link whatever between the Farran family of Dublin and the Farren family of Cork in spite of what has been written to the contrary. Maybe his father sent him there in disgrace after breaking his indenture.

When his apprenticeship in Cork was over, George set up there on his own and practised with reputation but if John Farran was relieved, it wasn't for long. "An early fondness for the drama induced him to quit that city and commence an actor in an itinerant company in England."[4]

George's choice of Liverpool where he arrived in the early summer of 1753, was a good one. In those days it was a flourishing seaside resort and a company of London players went up there every year when the London theatres were in recess, to entertain the summer visitors. The manager was William Gibson of Covent Garden.

George had nothing to recommend him except good looks and intelligence but he went to see if Gibson would take him on. The answer was "no" to which Gibson added that his company was full when he left London and that it was his unalterable maxim to reject superfluities of any kind. "I will not entertain more cats than can kill mice," he said.[6] Realising from George's manner and bearing that he did not come from theatre stock, Gibson tried to dissuade him from

16

going on the stage. ". . . the most prudent course for thee would be to push thyself into some other way of life which may support thee better. Whatever thy vain hope may flatter thee with, expect not to keep up long the flashy appearance thou dost now make shouldst thou engage with a travelling company of comedians." This advice fell on deaf ears and seeing he had failed, Gibson gave him a "present of half-a-crown (twelve and a half pence today) for a bed and supper. Thou dost look pitifully lank young man . . ."[6]

Perilously near starvation, George was obliged to join an inferior, strolling company with an exceedingly unpleasant manager called Shepherd. The company toured in England and Ireland and George's opinion of Shepherd is evident from this verse which he scratched on the window of his lodgings in Sligo.

> How different David's fate from mine,
> His blessed, mine is evil.
> His Shepherd was the Lord Divine,
> My Shepherd is the Devil.[7]

John Bernard, who tells the story, evidently visited Sligo after Elizabeth's marriage in 1797 for he goes on to say that he tried to persuade the owner of the house to extract the pane of glass as a souvenir for "the Countess of Derby." He met with a flat refusal, 'ever since Mr Farran scratched those lines I've nivver (sic) wanted for a lodger,' he said.

About a year after George's arrival in Liverpool he fell in love with the toast of the town, a fair-haired, blue-eyed beauty, Margaret Wright, a brewer's daughter. Her father had been very well-to-do but so lavishly hospitable that he had been obliged to sell his estate and had reduced his family to near-penury. What Margaret lacked in dowry she made up for in character and brought prudence and stability to what proved to be a very happy marriage. George and Margaret were married at St George's Church in Liverpool on New Years Day, 1755.

They were very young, George twenty-three and Margaret twenty-two. She was no actress but her love for George was strong and she joined Shepherd's company. They strolled with it together until they could afford their own Farran's Company. It was a rough, tough life and their first baby died. Their next, born on July 16th 1759, was Elizabeth, a lovely contented baby with beautiful big blue eyes. Three more children followed – George who died as a baby, Catherine (Kitty) and Margaret (Peggy).

John Farran, Elizabeth's grandfather died at Finglas, near Dublin in January 1765. He was unforgiving and described her father in his will as "my undutiful son, George."

Farran's Company was well thought of according to these extracts. The first is from The Georgian Theatre in Wessex.

> . . . Farran's company which was playing at Southampton in July with great success ("they far exceed all that ever acted here before") and on the 29th playing *The Jovial Crew* and *The Mayor of Garratt* before the Duke of Gloucester.[8]

James Winston wrote in the Theatric Tourist in 1805:-

> The first company of any note was that of Mr Farran . . . who performed at The Town Hall with considerable success, till 1766, when a regular Theatre was constructed and the management given to a Mr Johnson.[9]

With such complimentary notices, George must have been disappointed not to get the management of the new theatre but it did not stop him taking his company to Salisbury.

George Farran died in 1770. He was not an alcoholic as the scurrilous anonymous writer Petronius Arbiter declared, but a happy-go-lucky, convivial Irishman, "upright and honest, beloved by his family and friends and esteemed by his acquaintances."[10]

18

His death left his family almost destitute but Elizabeth, although only eleven years old "felt herself under a necessity of looking to some line of life, not only for the support of herself but of her mother and sisters."[11]

Chapter One – Footnotes

1. Farran. Dr Charles d'Olivier. Farrans of Six Continents (private typescript) p.6
2. Sheridan, Thomas. Life of Swift 1784 pp. 444-446
3. Farran. op.cit. p.8
4. Roach's Authentic Memoirs of the Green Room. 1796
5. Lewes, Charles Lee. Memoirs. 2 vols. 1805. Vol.2 p.17 et seq.
6. Ibid
7. Bernard. John. Retrospections of the Stage. 1830. 2 vols. Vol. 1 p.332
8. Hare, Dr Arnold. The Georgian Theatre in Wessex. 1958. p. 61, 62
9. Winston, James, The Theatric Tourist. 1805. p.64
10. Testimony of Truth to Exalted Merit. anon. 1797. p.8 (T.O.T.)
11. Ibid. p.11

Chapter Two

Where the family was when George died isn't known; it could have been Bath. Elizabeth and her mother are shown in the Orchard Street Calendar as members of the theatre company there for the season 1769-1770 and Elizabeth alone for 1770-1771. By 1773 they were in Chester where they had gone to see George's old friend, James Augustus Whiteley, manager of the largest circuit of provincial theatres in England, hoping he could employ them. He had no vacancies at Chester but he engaged the whole family for the Manchester season from December 8th 1773 to the first week in May 1774.[1]

Tate Wilkinson, the almost legendary manager of York Theatre reproduces this bill of the Farrans under Whiteley at Wakefield at Christmas 1773.

For this week only
At the Theatre in George-Yard
K.Hen.II or The Fall of Fair Rosamond
Singing between the acts
By Mrs Richards and Miss Farren
To which will be added, a New Pantomimical
Entertainment in the grotesque characters, called

OLD MOTHER RED-CAP

Mother Red-Cap	Mr Whiteley
Scaramouch	Mr Cummins
Hymen	Miss P. Farren
Servant Maid	Miss K. Farren
Columbine	Miss Farren

Masques in the Masquerade which followed
included Miss Farren and Mrs Farren.

Wilkinson said below it that he, "presents part of the bill as a curiosity and to see how merit sometimes rises and meets its due reward, as Miss Farren and her sisters were my opponents . . ."[2]

Elizabeth's reputation had preceded her to Wakefield which was agog with excitement at her arrival. The young bachelors besieged the box-office and one young articled clerk who had stopped to read an advertisement of the performance saw, coming out of the theatre, "the Columbine Queen, the most fairy-looking of youthful creatures, brilliant as spring and light as gossamer." She tripped into the street to go home after rehearsal. The road was icy and people were falling so several young men offered to escort the lovely girl. Seeing how this irritated her, the young clerk stepped forward, linking his arm in hers – it was young Mr Burroughs who had helped her three years before when her father was imprisoned in Salisbury. The two laughed merrily on recognising each other. He then escorted Elizabeth home.

The performance on Boxing-Night was a tremendous success and it was Mr Burroughs, now an incipient lawyer, who escorted Elizabeth and her mother to their lodgings.

While still in Manchester, Elizabeth's mother received this letter, undated.

> *Madam, – I have duly considered the subject of our late conversation and do not think there is the least chance of your deriving permanent benefit from theatrical pursuits. Inclination does not confer talent: for the sake of yourself and the children, I strenuously advise you to turn your attention to some other less dangerous and precarious way of life. I say less dangerous as applies to your daughters. I have passed a long career upon the stage, and where I have seen one person prosperous and happy, ten have failed, and many, particularly females have been morally cast away. If I had been bred a shoemaker or tailor, and had followed those humble callings with the same diligence as an actor, I should in all probability, be independent. Look around you in this busy town, and you*

will see hundreds of persons who were destitute as it were but yesterday, and are now on the highroad to wealth. Fix on some safe and certain occupation. Even a laundress, with tolerable plenty of work, is preferable to treading the stage as a make-weight. Do not feel offended at this bluntness. Nature has not endowed you with the qualities that are requisite to ensure success; as for Betsey, although she seems to possess every natural requisite, she is yet too young, and were she my daughter, I would sooner rear her up to go to service in a respectable family! Inclosed [sic] is a trifle of which I entreat acceptance. When the wheel of fortune takes a more favourable turn you may return it. I would advise you not to leave Manchester. It is a busy thriving town; let me hear your determination; and if you feel inclined to make any attempt in the way of trade, I will, with the utmost readiness, aid your views as far as my means permit.

Meantime with the utmost sincerity. I remain your friend. W.[3]

The 'W' remains a mystery. One is tempted to think it must stand for Whiteley but he was not considered to be sufficiently well-educated to be able to couch a letter in such terms. Whoever it was, he was not the only one to try to change Margaret's mode of life. The next letter from a woman friend came at about the same time and shows how deeply the stage moved people of the day, especially those with puritanical views.

. . . I am very sorry I could not speak to Kitty. I fear you will think I am too much like the rest of the world, a mere summer friend. If so, you do me great injustice, for I love you and respect you quite as well as when you were my equal in circumstances. My husband possesses all the essentials of a good and upright man; we have, as you know, a numerous family, and I am sure nothing would grieve you so much as to become the source of domestic uneasiness. To him I owe respect and obedience, and owing to your connection with the theatre, which he terms "Satan's Tabernacle" he has interdicted our intercourse. He is, as you know, a rigid

23

Calvinist, and of all people, hates players the most. To these circumstances, my dear Mrs F . . ., and not to diminished esteem, I implore you to attribute my not seeing Kitty last night. He is just gone on horse-back to Stockport and I embrace the opportunity of communicating this painful, yet, I also believe, not unexpected intelligence. I have explained how I am circumstanced as to the disposal of my private allowance. I am required to enter every little disbursement of alms, and where he disapproves, I dare not let the objectionable name appear any more. Our household accounts are balanced every week, and not a pint of milk or a bunch of greens, enters our kitchen but what is entered in our kitchen journal. I state these particulars to account for the paucity of my aid to you, my beloved school-fellow – when your wants are so pressing. It cuts my heart when I sit down to a plenteous table, and see my children all round me well fed, and well clothed, to think of you and yours. I asked him for a guinea this morning to give you. He said he should offend the Almighty by so doing! I shed tears, but they had no other effect than to excite reproof. I have, however, sent you a new Queen Anne guinea – a present from your dear father and mother who were my sponsors. Take it, use it therefore as your own. I intended it for you, and should have sent you two, if I had obtained the one I asked. When I reflect on the trivial amount of the help I can command, I blush to send it. I wish I might be able to persuade you to abandon altogether your dramatical prospects. Your daughters are, I know, educated too well for common servitude: but from what I hear and have seen of the misery to which players, both male and female, are so frequently exposed, I would prefer a decent and humane master for a daughter of mine than to allow her to become an actress. If you were to act thus, I should be permitted to assist you, and to an extent to be useful. Your daughters can each of them use their needles well, and are qualified to instruct others in everything that respectable tradesmen's daughters usually learn. What should you think of opening a school in Manchester? You know too well my husband is not the

24

only person to entertain a strong aversion to the society of players . . . Even Mr Younger, who seems to have everyone's good word, has a very limited number of real friends. And as to Mr Whiteley, you cannot be ignorant of the persecutions to which he has been subjected, and to the schisms which prevail, even in his own company.

I am thus earnest with you, because I love you. I fear you are depending on frail support. I cannot doubt but Mr R would let me take Kitty if you were to give up the Theatre altogether. It would be a source of the greatest felicity to be able to prove by my care of the child how dear you are to me. I should always have her at my side, and would treat her as if she were my own daughter. To find a situation for Betsey equally eligible might not be quite so easy; but you might keep her at home; if I might advise, I would place her as an apprentice to a mantua maker or milliner. She is a sweet girl, and has an address so genteel, and a manner so engaging that she could scarcely fail of doing well in either of those businesses.

I entreat you, my dear Mrs Farren to take this letter in good part, and when you have read it, fling it in the fire, for I would not willingly these sentiments should meet any eyes but your own. No, not even your daughters, for nothing less than the strong affection I bear you could have induced me to write thus freely of my husband. If you adopt my advice – you will remain in Manchester but free from all theatrical connections, and I will do my very utmost to assist your establishments.

If you pursue your favourite speculation, you shall have my ardent prayer for your welfare; and never shall want such help as my circumscribed means may allow me to afford. Once more – God bless you all, and believe me ever affectionately yours J.R.

PS I have sent a bundle herewith of which I treat your acceptance. [4]

What a fortunate thing it is that Margaret didn't destroy this letter as she was asked. It provides much information concerning not only her character and attributes but those of Elizabeth and her sisters. It also gives an insight into the excellence of Elizabeth's education and expertise as a needlewoman as well as confirming her sweetness of temperament. It comes as a considerable shock today to read of the measure of obedience and fear of an educated woman of her husband in the last quarter of the eighteenth century. Although both letters are undated the contents point to the spring of 1774.

Early in that year of 1774, the whole family took part in *The Merchant of Venice* and a masquerade at Manchester's Marsden Theatre on April 8th; Elizabeth was surprisingly billed as "Betsey"; it had been her father's nick-name for her. She sang a song to the accompaniment of a Mr Claggot on the guitar and spoke a poetic address and an epilogue written for the occasion by the famous actor, Samuel Foote.

Less than a month later, Whiteley dismissed the family *en bloc* which must have been a crushing blow although they would not be quite empty-handed. He had given Margaret a letter of recommendation to Joseph Younger, patentee of the Theatre Royal, Liverpool. It was Kitty's acting in the parts of "giddy girls" and chambermaids that Whiteley commended to Younger. Elizabeth was not mentioned, but it would be Younger who put her on her feet.

Younger was a splendid man. Not only was he a top theatre manager but he was kind and highly respected in Liverpool and had never been known to turn a deaf ear to a plea of poverty. As a manager and spotter of talent he could be mentioned in the same breath as Tate Wilkinson of York and at the time there was no higher compliment in the theatrical field.

The whole family was engaged to play at the Theatre Royal but it was no time before he judged Elizabeth to be a gem. She had an excellent memory, excellent powers of imitation, a sweet soprano singing voice and she was very versatile. In addition she was as pretty as a picture, had an elegant little figure and a warm and vivacious nature. Younger took her under his particular care and treated her as if she was his own child. He taught her and he trained her, his task being made easy by her quickness of perception and her ductile mind.

Elizabeth's mother taught her discretion, determination, strength of purpose and the value of punctuality – attributes which would never leave her. But she was no paragon. No easy task, particularly in the eighteenth century, to channel a high-spirited, attractive girl in the way she should go, let alone in theatrical circles. It is a credit to Mrs Farran that she succeeded and also to the fact that Elizabeth was no prig or bore but always gay and laughing and full of fun.

Money was short and it was hard on Margaret that she had to live in the poorest quarter of the city where her father had been in a position of respect. However low her surroundings she never sank below her natural level. As a contemporary put it, "she was possessed of an even temperament, gentleness and urbanity of manners forming a notable contrast to the people amongst whom she was forced to live."[5] This was a slum area in a house in Jackson's Row, next door to The Green Man public house. As far as kindness was concerned they had fallen on their feet for the owners of the house were Irish, a Mr and Mrs Stanfield (the parents of the scene painter Clarkson Stanfield, as yet unborn). Much later, when the financial tables were turned, Elizabeth never forgot how they had helped her mother and repaid them in kind.

Younger first cast Elizabeth in the part of Rosetta in *Love in a Village*, a comic-opera with songs written for it by Handel, Arne, Boyce and others of similar calibre. Although Elizabeth was not quite fifteen, she drew great applause. She had had earlier appearances but this could be counted as her stage début.

At the time, performers had to provide their own – and suitable – clothes for their parts but the Farrans were so poor this was not possible. Years later, Walker's Hibernian Magazine wrote, "but such was the poverty of her wardrobe that the ladies in the company, it is remembered, were obliged to subscribe each a proportion of apparel before she could be properly equipped; so much may great merit and superior talents be depressed by poverty."[6]

Her success as Rosetta gave Younger full confidence. He then cast Elizabeth in the taxing rôle of Lady Townley in *The Provoked Husband*. This she played as to the manner born, giving a foretaste as to what would be her *forte* in her career to come – playing the sophisticated "grande dame" of her day and Younger was so delighted with her performance that he gave her credit, "with all his tradesmen to procure any cloathes (sic) the family stood in need of."[7]

Elizabeth's successes were repeated in a number of provincial theatres. She was very versatile and played a number of Shakespearean parts. On one Christmas Eve in Chester (still with Younger) she was billed as Viola in *Twelfth Night* for her benefit and so was engaged in the unpleasant task of soliciting support, the custom at that time. She had received a rebuff from a clergyman and, as she turned from his door, she proffered her bill to an approaching horseman. He looked down on her and laughed with pleasure. It was young Mr Burroughs. This was their third unexpected meeting at Christmas. On reading the bill he promised her a full house for her benefit. He was as good as his word – the theatre was packed to the ceiling.

Younger kept a paternal eye on all Elizabeth's affairs and noted her financial circumstances. Whenever he thought it necessary, he advanced her salary so that the little family could live comfortably. She was an eminent favourite wherever she went and, "drew crouded (sic) audiences", her versatility being a great asset. Younger's company enlisted as much respect as any London company. He set a very high standard and the ambitious target of producing every play performed at Drury Lane and Covent Garden during the previous season which he usually attained.

During the summer of 1776, Younger's Company was playing in Birmingham. John Philip Kemble was already with it but now his eldest sister Mrs Siddons joined. She had been acting at Drury Lane for the season just ended, her first London experience and was expecting to return after the summer recess. In the event, shortly after her arrival in Birmingham, she heard from the Drury Lane prompter that she would not be needed any more. In her reminiscences she says she "went into a decline."

Her set down can hardly have been unexpected – London was not at all enthusiastic. After her appearance as Portia in *The Merchant of Venice* on December 29th (her first appearance in London) The Gazateer wrote, "there is not room to expect anything but mediocrity. Her figure and face, tho' agreeable enough have nothing striking; her voice . . . is far from favourable to her progress as an actress. It is also feared she possesses a monotony not to be got rid of . . ." From the time they first met at Birmingham, Elizabeth and Sarah Siddons became firm friends, a friendship which was approved of by Elizabeth's mother for in general, she discouraged her daughter from befriending players.

Younger's company returned to Liverpool in September where it was joined by Mr and Mrs Inchbald who also became life-long friends. They had just passed through a very lean patch, poverty being the common lot of players at the lower end of the profession. In her memoirs, Mrs Inchbald recalls that only a month before joining Younger, they several times went without dinner or tea and once went into a field to eat turnips they were so hungry.

In October 1776, Younger took the company to the new theatre in Manchester but was back in Liverpool before Christmas. On December 6th the Liverpool Advertiser announced, "the last night but Two, for the benefit of Mrs and Miss Farren, A Comedy . . . called *Love for Love.*" Elizabeth played Miss Prue, her mother the Nurse and her sister Kitty, Mrs Foresight. Five weeks later to the day, on January 10th 1777, Kitty died of consumption in Manchester where the company had returned after Christmas, remaining there until March.

On February 3rd 1777, Mrs Siddons acted the title role, *Seminaris* for Elizabeth's benefit. *Cymon* by David Garrick followed with Elizabeth playing Fatima and singing a song. Her weekly salary was the same as Mrs Siddons' and the top male actor – £1.11.6.[8]

29

Training for the theatre was unsurpassed in the provinces and by application and hard work, coupled with the help of Younger, before her eighteenth birthday Elizabeth had gained the only passport to success in London – a very high provincial reputation. Younger had her welfare at heart and, most unselfishly – for she was a great draw for his company – he recommended her to his friend, George Colman the Elder who had recently taken over the management of the Little Theatre in the Hay. He did secure the happiness of his Manchester public for Race Week which was outside the regular season.

> Miss Farren of our Theatre is engaged by Mr Colman to perform this Summer at the Theatre Royal in the Haymarket but has obtained leave of Absence for This Week that Performances intended for the Races may not meet with any Disappointments.[9]

With this firm booking to return for one week, Elizabeth, her mother and her remaining sister Peggy, left for London.

Chapter Two – Footnotes

1. Hare, Dr Arnold Hare. Theatre Royal, Bath: Orchard Street Calendar 1750 – 1805. (Bath. Kingsmead Press. 1977).
2. Wilkinson. Tate. The Wandering Patentee 1794. pp.200, 201
3. Broadbent, John R. Historical Soc. Lancashire & Cheshire Vol. LX1, 1910
4. Ibid
5. T.O.T. p.9
6. Walker's Hibernian Magazine. July 1794. Part II p.1
7. Ibid p.2
8. Price, Cyril. Theatre in the Age of Garrick. 1973 p.191
9. Hodgkinson, J.L & Pogson, Rex. The Early Manchester Theatre. Published for The Society of Theatre Research, 1960. p.89

Chapter Three

On arrival in London in May 1777, the newcomers took lodgings in Suffolk Street behind the Little Theatre which stood immediately on the left of the Theatre Royal in the Haymarket today. The latter was built to John Nash's design in 1821 and the Little Theatre was demolished shortly afterwards – in 1830.

For George Colman the Elder, the new manager of the Little Theatre, the odds were high against the success of his venture partly due to competition from the patent theatres of Drury Lane and Covent Garden but mainly on account of the isolated position. Most theatre goers lived in the centre of London and at the end of the eighteenth century, the Haymarket was right in the country making it necessary to traverse long, narrow and lonely lanes where they were often waylaid by footpads and thieves. Colman was well aware of the difficulties but determined to succeed. He realised he would have to provide first-class entertainment worth the hazards of the journey as well as putting on something out of the ordinary from time to time. First he had to attend to the theatre itself, improving, repairing, enlarging and decorating it as well as seeing to "certain decay'd and moth-eaten articles which were dignified by the name of wardrobe."[1] After this his essential need was to procure an outstanding cast. At that time, it was not the play which drew an audience but a particular performer. Thus players became veritable idols of the public, some of whom would see the same play many, many times for the delight of seeing a favourite player perform. This being so, Colman's son referred to his father's "revolutionary" plans for the Little Theatre writing that the main feature was "the formation of a Company of Performers to act in all branches of the Drama,"[2]

According to Town and Country magazine, Colman wisely offered "such advantageous terms that it is not to be doubted, he will be the commander of some good troops . . ." He also felt it an opportune moment to introduce new talent. Just then he received the letter from Younger, recommending Elizabeth. This led to her immediate engagement. At the same time, Colman promised to give small parts to her mother and her sister, Peggy.

In spite of straightened circumstances, Elizabeth is reported to have taken Younger's advice and waived "all immediate claim to salary on condition of being permitted choice of parts in which she thought it advantageous to appear."[3]

Colman also engaged two actors from Bath – a well-known stepping-stone to the London stage. They were John Henderson and John Edwin, both of whom became famous in a short time. The total number in the company was small and each performer would have to play many diverse parts.

The Little Theatre opened on May 15th 1777 with Colman's own play *The English Merchant,* which owed much to Voltaire's *L'Ecossaise* and was in fact dedicated to him. Afterwards came Garrick's revival of his Children's Dramatick [sic] Entertainment, *Lilliput.* This was very well received and Peggy took a small part.

Colman had made the mistake of opening before the recess of the patent theatres and so the audience was very thin, particularly as at the time, Drury Lane was packed out every night with the first production of Sheridan's comedy, *The School for Scandal,* with Mrs Abington, the reigning comedy star as the heroine, Lady Teazle. The takings of the first twelve nights amounted to just under £3,000, an enormous sum for the day.

It was a measure of Colman's scholarship that he had been asked to write the epilogue for *The School for Scandal* despite being the manager of another theatre – indeed he was considered to be the most brilliant epilogue writer of his day. It was spoken by Mrs Abington:

All this I told our Bard; he smil'd and said t'was clear
I ought to play high Tragedy next year
Meanwhile he drew wise morals from his play
And in these solemn periods stalked away
Blest were the fair, like you, her faults who stopp'd
And clos'd her follies when the curtain dropp'd
No more in vice and error to engage
Or play the fool at large on Life's great stage.

After the flop of Colman's opening night at the Little Theatre, he wisely closed down until the end of May when he opened again for three performances a week. From June 11th the theatre opened every night except Sunday until the end of the season.

Elizabeth's chance came on June 9th. An advertisement in the press stated that there would be a performance of Oliver Goldsmith's *She Stoops to Conquer* at The Theatre Royal in the Hay-Market on the following Monday. After the names of performers and characters *en bloc*, the next lines ran:-

Miss Hardcastle, Miss FARREN
(Being her 1st Appearance in London)[4]

and on the next day, Tuesday,

On 9th June, Miss Farren first appear'd in London, in the character of Miss Hardcastle in *She Stoops to Conquer* (or *The Mistakes of a Night*).

The part was admirably suited to Elizabeth's youth and vivacity and her reception was the antithesis of that accorded to Mrs Siddons. "She was stamped on the instant as a strong favourite with the public"[5] as one critic had it.

The next morning, Tuesday, June 10th under the heading Theatrical Intelligence in The Public Advertiser, the following appeared.

Last night the comedy of She Stoops to Conquer was performed at The Theatre Royal in the Haymarket, to a very numerous and respectable audience with great applause.

. . . Miss Farren was great beyond description, and her acting is alone sufficient to preserve this jumble of improbabilities and vulgarisms from the oblivion it deserves. From her acting last night, we may venture to pronounce her a very valuable acquisition to the stage; and under the direction of so able a manager as Mr Colman has proved himself upon every occasion, there is no doubt she will soon be of equal rank in the Theatre with the first of our comic actresses.[6]

Although Macqueen Pope said that Elizabeth, "swept to success" a great deal of application and hard work was needed before she reached the top of the theatrical tree. James Boaden had no doubt she would do so. He was at her début and nearly thirty years later wrote that Colman had, "possessed himself of a treasure essential to the style of his summer entertainment, and an actress able to divide the palm of genteel comedy with the elder Palmer," (an actor in Colman's company). "She was even then greatly admired and it was obvious that her lovely expression, her intelligence and the air of fashion about her would, at no very distant period, place her in the seat of Mrs Abington, when she should retire."[7]

Not all criticisms were so enthusiastic. "Her action not awkward and her delivery emphatic and distinct," wrote one, whereas the following proffers advice.

When . . . Miss Farren learns to tread the stage with more ease; to modulate and vary her voice; to correct in spirit and regulate her action; and to give proper utterance to her feelings by a suitable expression of voice and countenance, in our opinion she will be a most valuable acquisition to our London theatres.[8]

Any censure in no way disheartened Elizabeth but rather spurred her on to further effort. She had the intelligence to turn it to good account and try to improve the points mentioned. Encouragement came from the Morning Chronicle which observed that she was, "more perfect than most of the theatrical ladies who have been initiated into the profession in the country seminaries and has less ill habits . . ."[9]

Discussing the reviews after her début, John Galt wrote, "Considering the haste in which the morning criticisms on the theatre are written and the little time allowed to solicit the fittest phrase to convey the degree of merit that critics would express, it is still sufficiently obvious that her first appearance must have been highly satisfactory to the public and encouraging to herself."[10]

One criticism which Elizabeth took steps to remedy was the weakness of her voice but this was cured by singing lessons from Jonathan Battishill; no hint of this fault was levelled at her afterwards.

Having proved herself in a number of parts at the Haymarket during the summer of 1777, Colman entrusted her with Rosina in The Spanish Barber on 30th August. This was his trump card, his own adaptation of Le Barbier de Seville by Beaumarchais – the play on which Mozart would base The Marriage of Figaro in 1786 and which was to inspire Rossini's The Barber of Seville in 1816.

Colman had worked hard on The Spanish Barber setting great store by it. He felt it could become a lasting and lucrative attraction. The excellence of Elizabeth's acting greatly contributed to the success of the piece and the critics now credited her with genius. Garrick was in the audience on the first night and she also spoke his epilogue very well. Three days later he wrote to Colman.

September 2nd

I like your piece and that other most promising piece, Miss Farren – 'tis a shame that she is not fixed in London. I will venture my life that I could teach her a capital part in comedy, aye in tragedy too, that should drive half our actresses mad. She is much too fine stuff to be worn and

36

That was music in the ears of a young girl who was barely eighteen.

On September 12th there was a Command Performance of *The Spanish Barber*. This was the first of many times Elizabeth played before King George III and Queen Charlotte who were keen supporters of the theatre, especially of comedy. After the performance on September 16th, the "summer" theatre as it was often called, closed down until the following June but Elizabeth and her mother and sister remained in the south until the end of November 1777.

"Mr Colman's first season will cut a conspicuous figure in the history of the drama from the introduction of three performers; Mr Edwin, Mr Henderson and Miss Farren whose attributes will furnish conversation for years of futurity."[12] So Gilliland wrote in The Dramatic Mirror of 1808.

Elizabeth Farren
Miniature by Andrew Plimer Circa 1785

Elizabeth was lovely to look at. Tall with fair curly hair, arresting blue eyes and beautiful teeth which enhanced her merry smile. She had her fair share of Irish "come hither" – an over-abundance of attraction and charm combined with a winning personality. She was witty, she was humorous, she was fun to be with and the time had come for her introduction to High Society which she owed to her Irish background.

Her sponsor was Emily, Duchess of Leinster, known as "the Queen of Ireland". She knew the Dublin Farrans.

"Society in the eighteenth century was too full of pride and caste to open its door to the reigning goddess of the theatrical hour, unless that deity had evinced the possession of some of society's traits. Boaden praises Miss Farren for the innate delicacy with which she slurred many a risky passage in the old dramatists and it is easy to see from this that her elegance and refined taste, so far from being mere matters of acquirement through observation and contact, were intuitive and temperamental. Blood may not tell as strongly on the stage as on the race course, but nevertheless it counts. And be it known that Elizabeth Farren came of good sterling stock, a fine old Huguenot family . . ."[13] So says Dr W. J. Lawrence.

Very soon, Elizabeth's sponsor introduced her to her brother, the Third Duke of Richmond who invited her to become the supervisor of the private plays in his house in Privy Gardens, Whitehall. At Richmond House, she met everyone who was anyone. Many became her life-long friends, and two, her particular admirers: Charles James Fox, eminent statesman, rival of Pitt the Younger, and Edward, Twelfth Earl of Derby, said to be the best of all amateur actors.

The title of the first play which Elizabeth supervised at Richmond House isn't known but it is said that Lord Derby took a comic part and Fox was the stage-manager. Afterwards, Elizabeth, her mother and her sister returned to the north.

The new season at Manchester which began on December 9th saw Elizabeth with Younger's Company for the last time. In the following Spring, she had a great success as Cordelia in Shakespeare's tragedy, *King Lear*. At the end of the season she said goodbye to Lancashire and for the next nineteen years, until her retirement in 1797, she would be based in London.

Once more Elizabeth was at the Haymarket Theatre for the summer season of 1778. Fox had taken to following her everywhere – spending whole evenings dangling behind the stage, just for a look or a smile. Looking at portraits of him, it is hard to see how he was said to be irresistible to women, but Elizabeth proved the exception to the rule.

She did not like him. All the same it is to her lasting credit that she did not encourage such a very important man. Rumour has it that he proposed to her twice, she refused and he took himself off. Not long afterwards, he went to see Colman's new comedy *The Suicide* in which Elizabeth played a "breeches rôle", in other words, she wore men's clothes which were entirely unsuited to her elegant figure. After the performance Fox went to see Colman, 'Damn it Sir,' he said, 'she has no prominence before or behind, all is in a straight line from head to foot and her legs are like a sugar-loaf!'[14] Perhaps it was sour grapes but although she continued to play that rôle, the criticism prevented her from consenting to a breeches rôle ever again. This brings to mind the valid criticism that Elizabeth was too thin. Plumpness was admired in her day. "Her figure is not sufficiently muscular, were it a little more *embonpoint* it would be one of the finest in the theatre,"[15] wrote one critic. It contrasts oddly with a description of Mrs Siddons at a later date, "one of the finest [figures] on a stage and not at all inclined to *embonpoint*." It is hard to know who admired what.

If she had lost any esteem by the breeches rôle, Elizabeth quickly regained it by her acting in *The Provoked Husband* as Lady Townley when she played it for the first time in London in August 1778. This part firmly established her in the eyes of the public. The audience and actors were so enraptured by her performance that she was immediately engaged to play at Drury Lane the next season, as "first" actress in tragedy and "second" actress in comedy to the then reigning comedy star, Mrs Frances Abington – an unprecedented engagement. According to Mrs Mathews, "her career enjoyed uninterrupted prosperity"[16] from then on. Many years later George Colman the Younger would write, "To dilate upon the history of the lovely and accomplished Miss Farren would be very superfluous. No person ever more successfully performed the elegant levities of Lady Townly (sic) upon the stage or more happily practised the amiable virtues of Lady Grace in the highest circles of society".

Fox's departure made way for Elizabeth's other admirer, Lord Derby. He was a married man but his wife had run off with the Duke of Dorset so it wasn't in the least indecorous for him to be paying court to a beautiful actress. Every night he went to the theatre to see her act and then escorted her and her mother home after the play. For a time he was very despondent for all the notice Elizabeth would take of him was to give a polite little bow of good-night at her door. Eventually a platonic friendship which was to last for eighteen years, was formed. They never met except with a third person – usually Elizabeth's mother. This was not to say that the older woman was anything of a dragon for the two were utterly devoted – more like sisters than mother and daughter.

Although he was on the short side, Lord Derby was good looking. He had an oval face, high forehead, wide-set eyes, an elegant nose, good-tempered mouth and a firm chin. Three years before he met Elizabeth he had married Lady Elizabeth Hamilton, only daughter of the sixth Duke of Hamilton by his wife, Elizabeth Gunning – one of the notoriously beautiful daughters of John Gunning of Castle Coote, Co. Roscommon. These beauties took London by storm and it was quite common for people to climb on chairs to catch a glimpse of them walking in Hyde Park, the crowd was so great. Maria, the super-belle, had a guard of two sergeants and twelve men to keep the spectators at a suitable distance.

Lady Elizabeth Hamilton, Lady Betty as she was called, was not so beautiful as her mother but she was young and vivacious and took Lord Stanley's (as he then was) fancy. They became engaged though it had been engineered by the Duchess of Hamilton for Lady Betty was even then in love with the Duke of Dorset, who had gone abroad, seemingly forgetting her.

The Stanley wedding was fixed for June 23rd 1774. A fortnight before it, a magnificent *Fête Champêtre* was held by way of celebration. It was the first of its kind in England and took place on June 9th, at The Oaks, Lord Stanley's grandfather's estate near Esher, Surrey. Lord Stanley was heir to his grandfather, the Eleventh Earl of Derby, his father, Lord Strange, having died in 1771.

The Adam brothers designed the pavilions for the *Fête Champêtre*, David Garrick directed the players in the *Maid of the Oaks* (Lady Betty) by General Burgoyne, uncle by marriage of Lord Derby. The decorations were most elaborate costing £5,000 and Lord Stanley bought "all the orange trees round London,"[17]according to Horace Walpole. Nearly all the nobility went to it; the Prime Minister could not raise a quorum in the House of Commons so he wound up proceedings and repaired to the fête himself!

Mrs Delany called it, "a fairy scene". Writing to her on June 16th 1774, the Dowager Lady Gower gives this amusing side-light:

> All the world was there except ye Bloomsbury lot . . . I was told this day that ye old hoyden ye Duchess of Bedford was not at Ld Stanley's fete; I suppose piqu'd at his

recovering her niece's refusal so soon, for she w^d not let any of 'em go, tho' all ye Bloomsbury gange (sic) were invited. Since she has heard how fine, charming and elegant it was, she is silly enough to confess she repents . . . [18]

The Venetian Landscape painter, Antonio Zucchi, was commissioned by Lord Stanley to paint scenes of the fête on panels in the dining room of Derby House, Grosvenor Square, which was being built for him by the Adam brothers. Each figure in the paintings is a portrait and, whether walking or dancing, all the men are wearing hats. Zucchi's wife, Angelica Kaufmann also did decorative work in the interior of Derby House.

What an extravaganza! Such an entertainment caused a great sensation and is a good illustration of the sphere of elegance in which Lord Stanley moved. Only two years after their marriage, it was common knowledge that the young couple were at odds with each other. Lady Betty, though pretty enough, was wild and indiscreet and prone to escapades which injured the self-esteem of her husband. Her father, the Sixth Duke of Hamilton, was a dissipated rake who died from fast living. It seems his daughter was much the same. Her half-sister, Lady Charlotte Campbell gave this insight into her character. ". . . but a natural want of solidity of character, joined to a tender, artless disposition, left her an easy prey to folly and vice."[19] She was entirely pleasure-loving and spent many hours playing Whist for which she had a passion, often continuing until the small hours and playing for high stakes. Long enamoured of the Duke of Dorset who had returned from abroad for the *Fête Champêtre* especially to upset her it is said, her marriage was not on a firm footing. "Lady Betty certainly did not accept Lord Derby's offer of marrriage without affection but was persuaded into it,"[20] wrote Mrs Papendiek.

Lord Derby was an inveterate party-giver, a lavish and willing host and the contemporary gossip, George Selwyn wrote:-

42

Last night and the night before I supped at Lady Betty Stanley's. Their suppers are magnificent but their hours are abominably late.[21]

Presumably the Duke of Dorset was a visitor on many occasions. Georgiana, Duchess of Devonshire wrote that she looked upon him as the most dangerous of men for with that beauty of his, he was so unaffected and had a simplicity and persuasion in his manner that made one account very easily for the number of women he has had in love with him.[21]

At a ladies' cricket match at The Oaks where Lady Betty cut a pretty dash, this "ladies' man" was again attracted to her. "Alas! this beautiful Maid of the Oaks, after becoming wife and mother of a boy and girl, left her Lord and decamped with the Duke of Dorset."[22] (In fact she had had a second daughter, Elizabeth, whose father was the Duke of Dorset but she was left behind when her mother eloped and Lord Derby brought her up).

Lord Derby is best remembered today as a great sportsman and for his founding of the races the Oaks and the Derby – to the latter should be added, "as we know it," for it was James the Seventh Earl of Derby, Lord of Man, who established the Derby Stakes in 1621. This race was run on a narrow strip of land separating the bays of Castletown and Derby-haven on the Isle of Man and the Earl also contributed handsomely to the Derby Plate which was to be competed for at Easter each year. History does not relate for how many years it lasted. More than a century later, in 1780, the Epsom Derby Stakes was founded by the Twelfth Earl, supposedly at a dinner party. The conditions of the race were jointly agreed by Lord Derby and his close friend Sir Charles Bunbury, and the name of the race was to be that of one or the other founder. It was decided by the toss of a coin – so the Derby could have been the Bunbury!

Lord Derby often paid Elizabeth the pretty compliment of naming horses after her successful parts, (such as Hermione) and other parts

43

in her successful plays (Sir Peter Teazle). His other passion was for cock-fighting and he bred the crack cocks in England too – Black-Breasted Reds known far and wide as the "Knowsley Breed". Tenants at Knowsley were required to exercise young game cocks – this was written into their terms of employment. Lord Derby was known to have wagered as much as five thousand guineas on one cock-fight, and brought his cocks ready spurred to do battle into the drawing-room at Knowsley. He also kept a pack of stag-hounds at the Oaks but Surrey had no deer so carted animals were used.

Meanwhile Elizabeth's career progressed smoothly. Not long after her success as Lady Townley in *The Provoked Husband*, the manager's son George Colman the Younger – who spent a great deal of his spare time from Westminster School backstage in his father's theatre – noticed Elizabeth having a hot lunch of meat, vegetables and gravy. Every day he watched but he never saw it being brought in so determined to solve the mystery, he hid in Elizabeth's dressing room one day. At the appropriate time, he saw her mother delving deeply into the voluminous folds of her skirt and bringing out the meal. He showed himself and questioned her and she explained that she had had a tin pocket constructed in her skirt, "to stop the gravy from escaping". Thus she kept up her daughter's health, strength and good looks and ever afterwards young George Colman referred to Mrs Farran as "Mrs Tin-Pocket".

On September 11th Elizabeth played Rosina in *The Spanish Barber* for her very first Command performance before King George III and Queen Charlotte. On 23rd September came her first performance at Covent Garden when she played Clarinda in *The Suspicious Husband*. On September 30th she again played at Covent Garden, this time as Lady Townley in *The Provoked Husband*. Just over a week later, she would take her first curtsey at Drury Lane.

1. Colman, Geo. the Younger, Random Records 1830 p.229
2. Ibid.
3. Walker's Hibernian Magazine, July 1794 Part II p.1.
4. Boaden, James. Memoirs of Mrs Siddons 1826 p.69
5. T.O.T p.20
6. The Public Advertiser, June 11th 1777
7. Boaden. op.cit. p.69
8. Galt, John. Lives of the Players. 1831 p.229
9. Morning Chronicle, June 11th 1777
10. Galt. op.cit. p.229
11. Broadbent, J.R. Annals of the Liverpool Stage. 1908 p.63
12. Gilliland, Thomas. The Dramatic Mirror, 1804 Vol.i. p.121
13. Lawrence, Dr W.J. The Connoisseur. Feb.1911. Vol.XXIX. No.114 p.98
14. Dictionary of National Biography
15. T.O.T p.22
16. Mathews, Mrs Charles. (Anne) Tea Table Talk, 1839 p.34
17. Gentleman's Magazine as n.3
18. Delany, Mrs Mary, formerly Mrs Pendarves, née Granville. Life & Correspondence of: ed. Lady Llanover 2nd Series 1861. Vol 1/2 p.4
19. Piggott, Charles. The Jockey Club 1793 p.61
20. Papendiek, Mrs Charlotte. Court & Private Life in the time of Queen Charlotte, 1887 Vol.1 p.2
21. Cockayne. The New Peerage.
22. Papendiek. op.cit. Vol.1 p.149

Chapter Four

Elizabeth made her first appearance at Drury Lane on October 8th 1778, as Charlotte Rusport in *The West Indian,* by Richard Cumberland. Comments were generally favourable, the Evening Chronicle writing:-

> There was a good deal of ease in her deportment, and sufficient share of sprightliness and good humour, both in her delivery and in the expression of her features; indeed, if anything, too much of the latter as she wore a smiling face somewhat too often, and by never looking serious, destroyed in part the picturesque effect of the dramatic design of the author . . . she has no fault but that of being too flippant.[1]

This criticism was both encouraging and constructive; she righted the fault of flippancy which was never again levelled at her and played no less than eleven new characters in her first season at Drury Lane which would end in May 1779. From then on Drury Lane would be her base theatre.

Lord Derby continued to pay his attentions to Elizabeth. His wife remained living with the Duke of Dorset, while it was rumoured that she hoped to marry him. When Lord Derby was told this he at once said, 'then by God, I will not get a divorce; I will not give her the opportunity of using another man so ill as she has done me'. Lady Sarah Lennox, a sister of Emily, Duchess of Leinster, wrote to her friend Susan O'Brien on the same theme.

> It is no scandal to tell you it is imagined the D of Dorset will marry Ly D, who is now in the country keeping quiet and out of the way. There is a sort of party in town of who is to visit her and who is not, which creates gt. squabbles ...

but I'm told she has been and is still most thoroughly attached to the D of Dorset, and if so I should suppose she will be very happy, if the lessening of her visiting list is her only mishap.[2]

Naturally all society was interested in the scandal and Horace Walpole wrote to his friend, the British Consul at Naples, Sir Horace Mann:-

> The Duke of Dorset . . . is waiting for a Duchess until Lady Derby is divorced. He would not marry her before Lord Derby did and now is forced to take her, when he himself has made a very bad match. A quarter of our peeresses will have been wives of half our peers.[3]

In the eyes of the "ton", Lady Derby's crime was not that of bearing a child to someone other than her husband, but deserting her husband. This was considered to be unpardonable and resulted in Lady Derby being ostracised by many, including Queen Charlotte who forbade her the Court unless she returned to Lord Derby.

Before the Drury Lane summer recess of 1779, Elizabeth's last performance was as Louisa Freemore in *The Double Deception*. On May 27th she returned to the Haymarket where she negotiated quite a hurdle in her career on August 31st. Colman had engaged the Drury Lane comedy star, Mrs Frances Abington, to play the heroine Lady Newberry in his new comedy, *The Separate Maintenance* but she backed out at the last minute. Colman was now in a quandary. Good though she was, he thought Elizabeth too young and too inexperienced to fill the rôle but he had no alternative than to give it to her. To be fair, he alerted the audience in the prologue with, "A Younger Princess hoists the Empress' Flag". He need have had no qualms for Elizabeth acquitted herself with flying colours and the Morning Chronicle said, the occasion, "seemed to inspire Miss Farren with additional zeal."[4] This success would stand her in good stead in a year or so, and she played the part of Lady Newberry in *The Separate Maintenance* for her benefit – an extra night by permission

of the Lord Chamberlain on Friday, September 17th.

When she returned to Drury Lane for the start of the 1779-1780 season, Elizabeth found that her old friend Joseph Younger was now the stage-manager. Once more she reaped the benefit of his advice and help. As first actress in tragedy she gained merited applause. In comedy she stood next to Mrs Abington and had justly acquired the reputation of being a first-class actress.

On November 29th 1779, she scored a spectacular success in the tragic rôle of Hermione in Shakespeare's *The Winter's Tale* and had the honour of playing it at a Command performance before their Majesties on December 3rd.

This rôle brought a new experience for her – that of being painted in character. The artist was that past-master of theatrical painters, Johann Zoffany, who owed his success in that way because Garrick, (wanting prints for advertisement purposes), had encouraged him to sketch characters during actual performances. Zoffany sketched Elizabeth in the statue scene – the last scene in *The Winter's Tale*, which requires Hermione to remain still, supporting herself on a plinth. The portrait shows Elizabeth's very beautiful face but the statuesque pose looks strained and uncomfortable as no doubt it was. It was never exhibited although very highly praised. Charlotte Papendiek commented:

> Of Zoffany's representations of actors and actresses on a large scale, one of the finest is the full-length of Miss Farren as Hermione in *A Winter's Tale* . . . Zoffany seems to have painted at least two portraits of Miss Farren and to have been attracted by her charm and personality to a marked extent.[5]

At about the same time as Zoffany's portrait of Elizabeth as Hermione, Henry Bone, who later worked almost entirely in enamel, painted one of his rare miniatures on ivory of Elizabeth. Dr Williamson described it as, "a delightful portrait of a very interesting woman, because it represents Elizabeth Farren at the

49

time when she was in the hey-day of her popularity acting at the Haymarket and Drury Lane . . . There is no question about its authenticity. The features of the youthful artiste are quite unmistakable."[6]

During the eighteenth century there had been a distinct change in the tastes of theatre audiences. Shakespeare's plays were enjoying a revival and his comedies were much in favour since the 1740s. The plays most enjoyed in the last quarter of the century were those in which Elizabeth excelled – plays about life in High Society. Decency and delicacy – two of her particular attributes – were the hall-mark and part of the essential make-up of these comedies. Coarse humour was a thing of the past and this trend had been strengthened by the King and Queen who paid at least one weekly visit to the theatre.

Had the improvement in tone, manners and refinement not arrived, it would have been impossible for a virtuous woman to appear on the stage. It was well for Elizabeth she was born when she was and not a decade before, when as James Boaden said of Mrs Siddons, "her correct feeling might have kept her from the stage."[7]

Performers, being then all important, influenced playwrights to a marked degree and as the star could make or mar a play, authors tended to write with a particular player in mind. Until Hazlitt came along when criticism took on a new integrity, this attitude was reflected in reviews and seldom if ever in the late 1770s, did the play receive mention, let alone praise. Playwrights had no easy road. There was difficulty pleasing the middle-class section of the audience which caused an element of farce to be introduced into comedy which did not always make for a co-ordinated and balanced whole. Playwrights also had the management of the theatres to contend with and sometimes the whole concept of a play had to be altered while at others, a few small alterations would suffice. Sophia Lee's play, *The Chapter of Accidents* was a case in point. One part was based on a character in Diderot's *Le Père de Famille*. This was the crux of the trouble between Miss Lee and Mr Harris, manager of Covent Garden, to whom she had given it to produce. Just at that time, Harris had committed himself to producing another play which was also based on *Le Père de Famille* written by the actor Charles Macklin. Harris was afraid of quarrelling with Macklin who claimed to be "able to manage a quarrel better than any man." He had a disagreement with Miss Lee instead, who removed her play and gave it to George Colman at the Haymarket. To please him, Miss Lee adapted it to accomodate Elizabeth in the heroine's part of Cecilia. Colman then produced it with great success on August 5th 1780. It was highly popular through many seasons and Elizabeth was praised highly for her acting, "she was a fitting representative of the heroine . . . her conception and delineation of that interesting character surprised even her greatest admirers," wrote Mrs Mathews.[8]

On September 6th 1781, Elizabeth acted Cecilia in *The Chapter of Accidents* but five days later her part of Rosina in *The Spanish Barber* was taken by Mrs Hitchcock and her admirers were alarmed. Even more so when The Daily Herald gave the reason on September 13th. A threat had come to Elizabeth's career, her beauty, indeed her very life – she had smallpox. According to the paper she was confined to her home, 50 Great Queen Street, Lincoln's Inn Fields. Mercifully it was a mild attack and, nursed by her devoted mother, she was back on the boards of Drury Lane in less than three weeks. It was on October 2nd 1781 that she made her first appearance of the new Drury Lane season, once more as Charlotte Rusport in *The West Indian*. The house was packed, all anxious to see that their darling was unblemished. To all intents and purposes she was – any marks were invisible on the stage. However, four years later, six pock marks were still there and The Morning Herald[9] said that Lord Derby was transported by the delight of kissing them! It is a mystery how they knew.

On November 27th 1781, Elizabeth acted the heroine, Almeida, in *The Fair Circassian*, "a woeful tragedy" by Samuel Jackson Pratt. Lord Derby was a Whig and, in general, the party supported

Elizabeth – but not Sylas Neville, who said, "went to see the new Tragedy at Drury Lane *The Fair Circassian;* the Heroine by Miss Farren – old Drury has no other Tragic Queen at present and I can't say I admire her".[10] Next year he saw her again in *The Foundling* and wrote, "that insufferable piece of affectation, Miss Farren, was a tollerable (sic) coquette in Rosetta."[11] Charles Churchill agreed that he didn't like Elizabeth.

> affected, proud, conceited pert and vain
> as dead to feeling as alive to gain.[12]

Vanity may have led to the amusing caricature from *The Fair Circassian* which shows Elizabeth opposite Robert Bensley and carries this verse above.

> So Bensley stared with all his might
> E'en till his Eye-ball started
> So Farren flew to meet his Sight
> But she had laced herself so tight
> Her top and Bottom parted![13]

Was she in the habit of pulling her waist in to look even more sylph-like than nature had made her?

A while later this criticism appeared in The Morning Herald.

> Do not mistake for grace what an accidental spectator would call a broken back.[14]

No aspersions could be cast on Elizabeth's morals whatever else was said; she was chaperoned morning, noon and night by her watchful mother but her friendship with Lord Derby gave full rein to caricaturists. Henry Bunbury's, "When I followed a lass that was froward and shy . . ."[15] shows Elizabeth's coach disappearing out of the left of the picture, Lord Derby following post-haste on horseback. Bunbury's drollery was very acceptable in the last quarter of the eighteenth century for he was never political and seldom personal. He had however a fetish about horsemanship and gave Lord Derby a shocking seat on a horse in this caricature.

Shortly after its publication at the end of 1781, Augustus Hare wrote to Lord Carlisle, "The Caricature has had the good effect of mending his seat on horseback which is totally changed and consequently improved."[16] No doubt Bunbury felt his jibe had been justified.

Elizabeth's capacity for application and hard work was prodigious and although not at all robust, she must have had great stamina – and memory – to have weathered a programme of performances such as the following.

1781 The Haymarket.[17]

Tuesday, April 3rd.	Julia in *The Rivals.* (first time)
Tuesday, April 17th	Statira in *Alexander the Great.* (first time)
Monday, April 23rd	Sophia in *The Lord of the Manor*
Monday, " "	Emma in *Henry and Emma*
Tuesday, April 24th	Mrs Lovemore in *The Way to Keep Him* (first time)

Monday, April 30th	Sophia in *The Lord of the Manor*
Monday " "	Miss Tittup in *Bon-Ton*
Tuesday, May 1st	Juliet in *Romeo and Juliet* (first time)
Saturday, May 5th	Bella in *The Runaway*
Tuesday, May 8th	Cecilia in *The Chapter of Accidents*
Wednesday, May 9th	Dona Violante in *The Wonder* (first time)
Saturday, May 12th	Betty Modish in *The Careless Husband* (first time)
Tuesday, May 15th	Charlotte Rusport in *The West Indian*
Thursday, May 17th	Imoinda in *Oronoko* (first time)
Tuesday, May 22nd	Belinda in *The Old Batchelor* (sic)
Friday, May 25th	Ann Lovely in *A Bold Stroke for a Wife*
Wednesday, 30th May	Rosina in *The Spanish Barber*
Thursday, 31st May	Rosina in *The Spanish Barber*

Dissecting the above list it will be seen that Elizabeth acted sixteen different parts (seven quite new to her) in eighteen performances, and in two plays on two nights.

In the calendar of performances it is stated that *The West Indian* on May 15th and *The Old Batchelor (sic)* on May 22nd were both, "By particular desire of their Excellancies (sic) the Persian Ambassadors." The performance of *The Spanish Barber* on May 31st was a Command performance for King George III and Queen Charlotte.

Alterations and improvements to Drury Lane Theatre during the summer recess of 1782 cost £3,000. The boxes had been papered in "light pea green" and crimson curtains were hung on all doors with matching crimson baize on the seats – benches at that date. A few chairs were sometimes in the very front of one or two boxes.

All seemed prepared for the opening of the new season. Suddenly, Mrs Abington, the comedy star, demanded of Sheridan that she be paid £1,000 for the ensuing season. He flatly refused; he would see her further than meet such a demand and so she took herself off in high dudgeon to Covent Garden. Truth to tell, Sheridan was glad to see the back of her and her temperamental tantrums when box-office receipts were low, "false, treacherous . . . the worst of bad women"

Garrick had said of her. Besides, all through the previous seasons Elizabeth had been a very efficient second to Mrs Abington in comedy and, ever since her success as Lady Newberry in Colman's *The Separate Maintenance* which she had played with such aplomb, Sheridan knew she could step into Mrs Abington's shoes should the need arise. The comedy star had almost proprietary rights to many parts, thus Elizabeth's acting was now exposed to a severe test. However, she rose to the occasion and withstood the ordeal well.

On September 26th 1782, Elizabeth took her first curtsey at Drury Lane as Queen of Comedy. Also for the first time she played the part of Lady Teazle in Sheridan's famous comedy *The School for Scandal*. This was a part she would make peculiarly her own, upgrading Sheridan's whole concept of the character and changing it into the fashionable lady of the day.

Before the performance, the deputy manager read an address which Elizabeth had written in which she explained that she had undertaken to follow Mrs Abington, "by the encouragement of the manager," and not trusting in her own abilities, "she had taken every pains to qualify herself for this arduous task and that she therefore hoped for their indulgence."[18] She was never over-confident, always modest in spite of the praise showered upon her.

After her first performance as Lady Teazle, criticisms varied but all had at least a modicum of praise. From then on, all London was amazed at her success in the whole range of Mrs Abington's characters which hitherto even her greatest admirers had thought to be beyond her.

Her friend Mrs Papendiek did not allow their friendship to cloud her judgement. "Miss Farren, who now appeared in all Mrs Abington's characters, made a great step forward, for although no one could surpass Mrs Abington in the talent of enacting, the elegance of Miss Farren made her a general favourite. Her virtuous mind shone through her countenance and heightened the brilliance of her fine eyes, her naiveté being that of a chaste disposition and her manner that of a lady."[19] There were those who declared that

Elizabeth was a lady on the stage and an actress off it!

Mrs Charles Mathews contrasted Elizabeth and Mrs Abington in these words, ". . . she took over the range of characters in comedy with extraordinary ability. Miss Farren, as it afterwards proved, needed no guide to excellence but her own judgement: and it may be questioned whether in point of personal elegance and innate refinement, The Farren did not exceed The Abington. Equal in grace, superior in beauty to her accomplished predecessor, she possessed all her power – if we except that of reflecting vulgar life, to which Miss Farren's natural refinement could not have merged into the coarseness of . . ."[20] Here Mrs Mathews refers to two parts so vulgar that they were outside Elizabeth's scope – she who had been called, "the camellia of the conservatory, soft, beautiful and delicate."[21]

Horace Walpole thought little of *The School for Scandal* but he thought well of Elizabeth's acting and wrote to the Countess of Upper Ossory.

> In distinction of manner and refinement she excelled Mrs
> Abington who could never go beyond Lady Teazle which is
> a second rate character . . . that rank of women are always
> aping women of fashion without arriving at the style.[22]

Here Walpole was sniping at Mrs Abington's background; she had been an errand girl and a flower vendor on the streets.

A fortnight after Elizabeth's first appearance as Queen of Comedy at Drury Lane, Mrs Siddons returned to London. She had spent the intervening six years since her set-down of 1776, with the best of the provincial managers including Younger of Liverpool, Tate Wilkinson of York and Palmer of Bath. From her first appearance on October 10th 1782 as Isabella in Garrick's adaptation of Southerne's tragedy, *The Fatal Marriage*, in the same theatre where she had been said to have no promise, she went from strength to strength reaching the peak of her fame as Lady Macbeth.

With an eye to keeping up his policy of providing unusual

entertainment at the Haymarket, Colman put on something quite out of the ordinary in June 1784 – *The Election of the Managers*, a skit on the recent General Election. Since the act of 1737, every play had to obtain a licence from the Lord Chamberlain and Colman had had a great struggle to get *The Election of the Managers* passed by the censor – there were too many allusions to real life personalities. Elizabeth took one of the two female parts, both of which had real life prototypes. One was the Duchess of Devonshire, who was very wild and impulsive and while canvassing on behalf of Elizabeth's erstwhile admirer, Charles James Fox, she became notorious for securing votes with kisses! With such extraordinary electioneering, Colman had full scope for a political burlesque and it should have been a great success – so it would have proved had it not been for a single member of the audience.

To start with, this clever and original satire had a favourable reception but due to the persistent objections of Bob Monckton, it ended in a flop. Bob Monckton was the son of General Monckton who had fought with Wolfe at Quebec. Every night, this big, fat man sat alone in his box at the Haymarket watching *The Election of the Managers* and shouting, "Off, off" throughout the performance. Strange to relate, he was not ordered out of the theatre and his opinions became infectious, for each night more of the audience joined in until in the end, the whole audience was clamouring its disapproval. There was nothing for it but to take the play off.

Three months after this Elizabeth must have felt a deep sadness at the loss of her dear friend and mentor, Joseph Younger, who died on September 3rd. To him she owed her stage training and her introduction to London. Without him she would have got nowhere. He was only forty-nine when he died. James Boaden wrote, "he was a gentleman of considerable talent . . . sound judgement and very extensive knowledge."[23]

The Marriage of Figaro by P.de Beaumarchais had been produced most successfully in Paris and Thomas Holcroft with a Monsieur Bonneville, abridged and adapted it into a three act comedy, *The*

Follies of a Day or the Marriage of Figaro which was put on at Covent Garden on December 14th with Elizabeth as Susan. What happened could have led to disaster but for great presence of mind of the actor, Bannister. John Adolphus tells the tale.

> Miss Farren, whose grace and charms gave the highest finish to Susan, standing near one of the sidelights, set on fire the mantilla of light gauze which descended from her head to the lowest part of her dress. Bannister, perceiving the accident when no one else did, approached without alarming her, enveloped her in his Spanish cloak, and by the pressure of his hands, extinguished the flames. Thus his presence of mind prevented great alarm in the elegant actress and her friends and the thanks he received were liberal and unbounded. [24]

Unlike the versatile Elizabeth whose acting in tragedy had been praiseworthy and of a high standard, Mrs Siddons was unable to change to the sphere of comedy; Bannister said a smile, "was not habitual to her"[25]and that her comic acting never pleased him. This was well illustrated on January 27th 1785 when Colman supplied the epilogue to a revival of Massinger's *Maid of Honour*. Mrs Siddons played the Maid with grace and sweetness but she tried in vain to give comic effect to Colman's epilogue. Her gaiety did not excite mirth – it was patience smiling at grief, the condescension of tragedy. The critics of the day were unanimous that it would be better to trust such things to Miss Farren.

Elizabeth's failures were those few times when she was miscast. Such was her part as Mrs Charles Euston in Mrs Inchbald's comedy, *I'll tell you What* which was put on at the Haymarket in August 1785. Writing to Mrs Inchbald a fortnight later, Francis Twiss, (the compiler of a Verbal Index of Shakespeare's works, widower of Mrs Siddons' sister) gave Elizabeth a vicious slating. Of the acting he wrote, "I can at present only say that the chief part deserved praise; always however excepting Miss Farren, who is beyond description despicable. Such playing, however is beneath criticism and I shall dismiss it immediately."

Boaden at once sprang to Elizabeth's defence:-

> The *comedie larmoyante* was not suited to her. Nature had dressed her countenance in *smiles*, and her beautiful features looked *sullen* in grave expression. But a graceful figure, fine manners, good sense, and the practice of the stage must always save their possessor from being *despicable*. Her comedy, though not near Mrs Abington's in the *beau monde*, was far superior to anything else, and displayed *gaiety* of refinement.[26]

Three years before, General Burgoyne had written in the preface to his *The Lord of the Manor*, that the English public went to the theatre to be amused and not to see scene after scene of "tenderness and sensibility" of which *comedie larmoyante* consisted.

In spite of all this, there was a most enthusiastic account of the last performance of *I'll Tell You What* together with the "lively and elegant" after play, *Here and There and Everywhere*. In the papers the morning after (September 14th 1785) and on the day itself, the Morning Chronicle sported the following on the front page.

Lines Addressed to Miss FARREN

When Farren's loveliest form I view'd,
A form that's so divine!
Her charms, ye godd's my heart subdu'd,
Which heavenly charms outshine

Oh! how I look'd and gaz'd to see
Such transport here on earth
Love, mighty Love, enraptur's me;
And she in heaven had birth!

Yes, I'm in love, nor words, my dear,
Can what I feel declare,
Somehow (I'll tell you what) 'tis – Here
And There! And Everywhere! [26]

On September 16th the Morning Chronicle reported ". . . last night the manager of the Haymarket Theatre closed his triumphal campaign, honoured with a most brilliant and numerous audience, who expressed the utmost satisfaction . . . the deservedly successful plays of *I'll Tell You What* and *Here and There and Everywhere*." So much for Mr Twiss's adverse comments on Elizabeth's acting.

Although glowing reports were in the majority, the press never hesitated to criticise when it was deemed necessary as illustrated in the following review of *All in The Wrong* in the Morning Chronicle.

> Miss Farren's Belinda, though not all perfection, did her great credit. Her outline of the character was delicate, masterly and striking; and there wanted but a few touches of nature to make the colouring correct. In almost every one of her scenes with Beverley, she was playful, expressive, and interesting. She should have showed more anxiety and was a trifle artificial. We point out these trifles because generally we regard Miss Farren as an actress of uncommon merit, and because we think her Belinda is so good, that we wish it to be entitled to praise without exception.

That was in October 1785 and The Morning Chronicle on November 1st gave this comparison of Elizabeth and Mrs Abington.

> Miss Farren is generally considered as the rival of Mrs Abington. We think however that a very distinguishing part of her merit lies in a cast of characters, wholly out of Mrs Abington's line; in characters where there is a considerable mixture of the grave with the gay. In these Miss Farren is without competitor

Just such a part was Constantia in *Comedy Chances* for which Elizabeth gained much kudos. She then had a short bout of illness. At the end of November she played the Widow Belmore in Murphy's *The Way to Keep Him*. "Miss Farren's The Widow Belmore is a very capital performance . . . It is a comforting reflection to all who delight in comick (sic) representation, that we have so young, and beautiful an actress, who comes so near Mrs Abington in talents, and who promises to be equal to that all accomplished comedian, in the exhibition of ease and elegance of manners and deportment, and in the display of graceful levity, modest mirth, and polished humour."[28]

Elizabeth was too thin – The Prince of Wales would certainly have thought so – but she was clever at disguising this short-coming. "Miss Farren was in the perfection of her charms; her figure was above the middle height, graceful and suited to the disposition of drapery which served to conceal the lack of plumpness which was her only defect; her eyes were blue, she had a lovely mouth and winning smile, her voice was sweet . . . ," wrote one critic and another, "Her figure is . . . of that slight texture which allows and requires the use of full and flowing drapery – an advantage of which she knows well how to avail herself." As the New Monthly Chronicle summed her up, "a more pronounced exhibition of grace and all round accomplishment never presented itself to the view of an audience."

Richard Cumberland wrote *The Natural Son* with Elizabeth in mind as the heroine, Lady Paragon.

> I flattered myself that in the sketch of Lady Paragon I had conceived a character not quite unworthy of the talents of Miss Farren . . . So exquisite was the style in which Miss Farren gave her character its best display and so respectful were her auxiliaries . . . that they could never deprive the comedy of favourable audiences.[28]

Here Cumberland is attributing the success of the play to the excellence of the performers. Some years later his play *The Country Attorney*, led to trouble with Elizabeth.

Elizabeth considered the heroine's part of Lady Rustic in *The Country Attorney* to be beneath her and she refused to act. Cumberland and Colman were dependant on her and to make matters worse, Colman was ill at the time which left Cumberland to deal

Ramberg delt.　　　　　　　　　　Grignion & Bartolozzi sculpt.

MISS FARREN in OLIVIA.

with the trouble. Telling Colman that Elizabeth was a spoilt child who had done them much mischief, he wrote an undignified letter to her beginning, "As you are born to have all mankind at your feet, you will not refuse the addresses of an old poet, who is as much devoted to your fame as any man could be"[30] Elizabeth's response shows the sway a top-flight actress could have over a playwright and a manager, as Cumberland's letter to Colman shows.

> My Dear Sir,
> I have just received your letter signifying Miss Farren's commands for transposing her introductory scene to the second act; be it so, but I conclude it will be done with the hand of a master, or you will transpose it yourself, therefore I rest in peace. For heaven's sake, write her an Epilogue. I have plunged from thought to thought in the profound of nonsense, and can fix on nothing; one sense is left me, the sense of your kindness.
>
> Farewell.
> R.Cumberland.[31]

The Country Attorney was produced but according to Boaden, it was very coldly received and did not merit "any particular remark". Cumberland must have watched his step with Elizabeth afterwards.

To enumerate Elizabeth's successes would be inappropriate. She kept her versatility not confining herself to the "genteel" comedies which were her particular sphere and in which she was an overwhelming success. There were many Shakespearean rôles in her repertoire in comedy and tragedy and she won popularity by her acting of Emmeline in a shortened version of Dryden's masque, King Arthur. J.P. Kemble played the king and Thomas Stothard painted a portrait of the two of them in character. There is also a painting of this masque by Wheatley which includes William Brereton as Oswald and Francis Aickin as Merlin in addition to Kemble and Elizabeth.

Other paintings of Elizabeth in character include her as Penelope in *The Gamesters* by De Wilde and as Olivia in *Twelfth Night* and Hermia in *A Midsummer Night's Dream* by T.C.Ramberg. In the latter, the artist chose that moment when Hermia starts from sleep, calling out:-

> Help me, Lysander, help me; do thy best
> To pluck this crawling serpent from my Breast[32]

No wonder Elizabeth looks so wild and unlike herself. There were also many portraits and drawings by unidentified artists.

An artist who preferred to paint Elizabeth as her lovely self was a protegé of Sir Joshua Reynolds, Ozias Humphrey, who was much patronised by the Royal Family. He was so popular and sought after that after one Royal Academy exhibition he wrote to his brother, that he had had to give up the daily newspaper as he found it "amazingly interfered" with his painting adding, "when the hurry is over I hope to be able to subscribe to it again."

While Humphrey was painting a miniature of Elizabeth in 1785, Lord Derby wrote these lines to him.

> O thou, whose pencil all the graces guide
> Whom beauty conscious of her fading bloom,
> So oft implores alas! with harmless pride,
> To snatch the transient treasure from the tomb!
> Pleas'd I behold the fair whose comic art
> Th' unwearied eye of Taste and Judgment draws;
> Who charms with nature's elegance the heart
> And claims the loudest thunder of applause.
> Such, such should prompt thy pencil's toil;
> Of serving folly give thy Labour o'er;
> Fools never will be wanting in our isle,
> Perhaps a Farren may appear no more.[33]

Chapter Four – Footnotes

1. Evening Chronicle, October 10th 1778
2. Lennox. Lady Sarah. Life & Letters of. ed. Ld Ilchester & Ly Stavordale 1901 p.290
3. Walpole, Horace. To his friend Sir Horace Mann, January 29th 1779
4. Morning Chronicle, September 1st 1779
5. Papendiek. op.cit. Vol.2 p.175
    This quotation from Manners & Williamson's book, Zoffany comes in the memoirs of Charlotte Papendiek. p.198. At Court as Assistant Wardrobe Keeper to Queen Charlotte, she was in a position to learn much about the Royal Family and high society which makes her observances particularly valuable. Never intended for publication, her memoirs were written down in 1831 to pass the time during a tedious convalescence at the instigation of her children. This lapse of time between recording and the events themselves, accounts for certain discrepancies in dates.
6. Williamson, Dr., The Connoisseur April 1909 Vol. XXIII No.92 p.6
7. Boaden. op.cit p.6
8. Mathews, Mrs Chas. (Anne) op.cit. p.40
9. Morning Herald , October 29th 1785
10. Neville, Sylas. 1767-1788 Diary of; (1950) O.U.P. ed. B Cozens-Hardy 1950. p.285.
11. Neville, Sylas. op.cit. p.292.
12. Churchill, Chas. *New Rosciad* 1844
13. Prints & Drawings Room, B.M.
14. The Morning Herald, 29 October 1785
15. Prints & Drawings Room, B.M.
16. Prints & Drawings Room, B.M.

17. Performances and comments taken from The London Stage, 1660-1800 Part 5 Vol.1. Theatrical Season 1780/1781 ed. Charles Beecher Hogan, University Press, Carbondale, Illinois, 1968

18. Papendiek. op.cit p.67

19. Ibid. Vol. I p.250

20. Mathews op.cit. p.40

21. Galt op.cit. p.229

22. Powys, Caroline. Passage from the Diaries of Mrs Lybbe Powys, ed. E.J. Clemenson 1899, Vol II p.30

23. ˙ Boaden, James. 1833

24. Adolphus, John. Memoirs of John Bannister 1839,p.136

25. Campbell T. Life of Mrs Siddons , 1834, p.111

26. Boaden, James. Memoirs of Mrs Inchbald, 1833 p.72

27. Morning Chronicle, September 14th 1785

28. Ibid, November 1st 1785

29. Cumberland, Richard. Memoirs, 1806 p.483

30. From Cumberland, Richard to E. Farren, 30th June 1787

31. From Cumberland to Colman to Colman the Elder

32. Shakespeare, A Midsummer Night's Dream Act V, Scene 2.

33. Lord Derby to Ozias Humphrey. T.O.T p.33

Chapter Five

Actors are indubitably the legitimate property of the public.[1]

Although Mrs Mathews wrote this line in the 19th Century, it was as true a century earlier as it is today; players and their affairs are considered common property. This being so, the unusual nature of Lord Derby's relationship with Elizabeth caused much interest and many a raised eyebrow. Loose morals were the order of the day pervading all walks of life. In the lower classes, gin drinking and overcrowding were contributory to laxity in sexual relations and stage circles had a bad name. This was accentuated by brothels often being attached to theatres. A platonic friendship with an actress – or anyone else – was almost unheard of. Mrs Papendiek tells that Lord Derby had once taken a step very much in the wrong direction.

> The Earl of Derby made her an offer of protection, which she immediately convinced him it was not her disposition to accept.[2]

Elizabeth was hurt and surprised that Lord Derby had misjudged her. He was by no means her only admirer and she thought she had made it quite plain that friendships were to be platonic or not at all. As Macqueen Pope has it, "A vast crowd of lovers was sighing at her feet, but she remained immaculate . . ."[3] No guilty splendour for her – she would be no man's mistress. And so, for quite some time, she made Lord Derby eat very humble pie indeed. After he had realised the enormity of his *faux pas*, he set about putting things to rights.

> He then begged that she would agree to marry him on the death of his wife, who was in ill health. This she in part accepted, but on condition that he would only see her in company, as she was determined to pay every attention to

her profession for the support of herself, her mother and her sister, and to preserve her character inviolable. Lord Derby agreed, but insisted on her using his carriage. That she also refused, but at least it was settled that a coach, with every appendage for travelling, and for London work, should be kept for her in my lord's mews; that two footmen should attend, and if at any time pecuniary assistance should be required, that she should apply to him only as a friend. No jewels or presents were to be offered, and every decorum to be observed, that, should they live to be united, she might be respected.

To this, Mrs Papendiek added, "Dear, sweet, amiable creature! Indeed she lived up to her determination."[4]

From then on, Lord Derby and Elizabeth could be considered as formally engaged. Cold blooded as it may seem he had regularised her position as far as it was in his power and on her part, Elizabeth had taught him a lesson that she would remain a virgin until her marriage. It was frequently stated that she never went anywhere without her mother. As Mrs Papendiek put it, "her mother with whom she lived in the closest affection used to accompany her daughter to the theatre, and her presence would help Miss Farren to decline overtures of those performers whom, without wishing to offend, she would gladly avoid."[5] Universally it was stated that the only uninterrupted interviews Lord Derby had with Elizabeth were in the screen scene in *The School for Scandal*.

Frances Williams Wynn was a young girl at the time and later wrote, "I recollect [not the admirable acting in the famous screen scene but] the circumstances of seeing Lord Derby leaving his private box to creep to her behind the screen; and of course we all looked with impatience for the discovery, hoping the screen would fall a little too soon and show the audience Lord Derby as well as Lady Teazle."[6]

Having refused to divorce his wife when she wanted it, Lord Derby would have liked a divorce now himself but it was too late. The Duke of Dorset had deserted Lady Derby and was married to another; his lordship must "consequently await the awful event. Meanwhile the son and daughter profited by her care and tuition; and so great became the affection of Lord Stanley for her, that he even, if had been possible, would have gladly been united to her." Mrs Papendiek's memory has certainly played her false here – Lord Stanley was only twelve years old at the time! However this discrepancy does not diminish the strong affection he and his sister Lady Charlotte, bore Elizabeth.

No shafts of malice appeared to penetrate Elizabeth's armour of respectability or alter her acceptability when, "it was an undisputed fact that she never admitted His Lordship unless Mrs Farren was present."[7] The permanent gooseberry! There were no imputations on her fair fame but caricatures on the friendship continued, some very cruel but outwardly at least, Elizabeth seemed to be impervious. Neither did she heed some verses which attempted to dissuade her from having anything to do with her noble *inamorato* adjuring her not to play "Darby and Joan" too soon. This on the pretext that she was yet too young. She was discreet and sensible and gave no satisfaction to those keen observers who watched her every move hoping she would put a foot wrong and anxious to magnify any little foible and turn in into a deformity. In this she disappointed them. As Boaden said, "Sensitive delicacy was her distinctive character and also the propriety of her private conduct." Whatever was said, Elizabeth was secure in the affection of her many friends and what was more, of Lord Derby's relatives.

Elizabeth was a finished pattern of elegance and fashion and she now [during 1786] decided the time had arrived to move from Queen Street, Lincoln Inn Fields, to an area more in line with her eminence in society. She chose Bow Window House, Green Street, Mayfair, a fashionable quarter, then on the outskirts of London, so isolated that Horace Walpole said it was quite unsafe to go out after dark without his blunderbuss for protection. He lived in nearby Berkeley Square.

Mayfair was the centre of the square mile inhabited by "the Ton" or High Society. Lord Derby lived in Grosvenor Square in beautiful Derby House (No.26), a site now occupied by the American Embassy, which between 1773-5 was, "given the interior that has made Derby House famous." This was done for Lord Stanley as he then was, (under the supervision of his uncle by marriage, General Burgoyne), by Robert Adam who left the exterior with its bowed balconettes much as it was but added a Doric portico and extended the rear wing. Extensive decorations by Angelica Kaufmann – the doorheads for instance – and her husband Antonio Zucchi, were carried out after Lord Stanley and Lady Betty married in 1774. In September that year, Adam designed a remarkable domed twin bed to occupy a round "toped" (sic) alcove in the first floor chamber.

At least one writer approved of Elizabeth's move, "Why not? an ampell (sic) income for talents exerted for their amusement might fitly be enjoying a style of elegance. She drove from her house, in her own chariot, to the theatre."[8]

No longer was the fare for friends the simple shoulder of mutton, baked potatoes and porter of Suffolk Street; an elegant house called for an elegant table at which to entertain, "the first characters of the beau monde." Invitations to Elizabeth's after-the-play suppers were eagerly sought. Her mother presided and Lord Berwick wrote:-

> Ah, those charming suppers in Bow Window House where I was admitted when I was a very young man, and where one used to meet General Conway and Lady Ailesbury, Mrs Damer and the old Duchess of Leinster, the Ogilvies; General Burgoyne, Fitzpatrick . . . and all the pleasantest people in London.

Those mentioned are in the "Ton" and Elizabeth had met them at Richmond House. Lady Ailesbury kept her late husband's title although married to General Conway. Her daughter Mary by the Third Earl of Ailesbury, was now Duchess of Richmond; the Duchess of Leinster had also kept her title. She was now Mrs William

Ogilvie having married the tutor to her Fitzgerald brood.

Horace Walpole was a frequent guest at Elizabeth's suppers. He and Lord Derby were very close friends. Not only had Walpole crowned Elizabeth "Queen of Comedy" and said that she was the most perfect actress he had ever seen, but writing to the Countess of Upper Ossory he referred to her as, "the first of all actresses".[9] He kept a miniature of her at Strawberry Hill, his house at Twickenham. (This miniature was bought by Elizabeth's daughter, the Countess of Wilton at the sale of Walpole's effects in 1842, for £16.16.0d).

The Hon. Mrs Damer, mentioned as a supper guest, was General Conway's daughter by Lady Ailesbury. Since widowed in 1776, she had devoted herself to literary and artistic pursuits. Walpole said, "she models like Bernini" and she became a renowned sculptress. Dr Erasmus Darwin wrote of her;-

> Long with soft touch shall Damer's chisil charm
> With grace delight us and with beauty warm.[10]

Travelling on the continent, Mrs Damer met Napoleon and promised him a bust of Charles James Fox. She kept her word and in return, Napoleon gave her a gold snuff-box with his portrait in diamonds which is in the British Museum.

It must have come as a shock in those days to learn that the Hon. Mrs Damer was, "a Lady much suspected for liking her own sex in a Criminal Way". Later in the same passage Mrs Piozzi wrote, "'tis grown common to suspect Impossibilities (such I think them) whenever two ladies live too much together. Its odd ye Roman Women did not borrow this horrible vice from Greece – it has a Greek name now and is called Sapphism . . ."[11]

Mrs Damer executed a beautiful marble bust of Elizabeth as Thalia, the Muse of Comedy, now in the National Portrait Gallery which led Mrs Piozzi to note disapprovingly that she, "had Miss Farren the fine comic actress often about her last year; and Mrs Siddons's Husband made the following lines on them."

Her little stock of private Fame
Will fall a Wreck to Public Clamour,
If Farren leagues with one whose Name
Comes near – Aye very near – to Damn her[12]

'Keep Mrs Damer at Distance,' ordered Lord Derby!

With her charming personality and joie de vivre, Elizabeth was excellent company and as popular a hostess as a guest. A "fascinating woman", Mrs Mathews called her adding, "ladies of rank and character received and visited her on the most familiar terms of friendship and daily extended the circle of her distinguished friends."[13] Mrs Papendiek, so closely allied to the Court, wrote that they, "continued to have the enjoyment of Miss Farren's society in private."

Mrs Siddons moved in the same social sphere but her entertainments were less intimate and very ostentatious – not approved of by the public as this extract from the Public Advertiser of February 3rd shows.

. . . the common weal may suffer too much from the frequency and luxury of this lady's banquets . . . What would become of oratory, should Mr Sheridan the elder die of repletion at her table? What a mortal blow would the law receive, if the faculties of Mr Erskine were "whelmed' under a mass of her tempting viands?" And could the art of painting have survived the loss of Sir Joshua Reynolds, had he died of indigestion of the profuse supper she lately gave him? Let Mrs Siddons therefore be told that as often as she throws out these unsalutary lures to her friends, she sins inexcusably against the interests of the public, She may be pardoned for being too regardless of her own.[14]

Fanny Burney admired Mrs Siddons on the stage and looked forward to meeting her in person but she was disappointed.

Mrs Siddons manners, quiet and stiff, in voice, deep and

dragging; and in conversation formal, sententious, calm and dry. I expected her to have been all that is interesting; the delicacy and sweetness with which she seizes every opportunity to strike and captivate on the stage persuaded me her mind was formed with that peculiar susceptability which in different modes, must give equal powers to attract and delight in common life. But I was very much mistaken. Whether fame and success have spoiled her, or whether she only possesses the skill of representing and embellishing materials with which she is furnished by others, I know not, but I still remain disappointed.[15]

Superb actress as Mrs Siddons was, Fanny Burney was not alone in her opinion. Sheridan must have agreed with her for him to have made the remark, "make love to Mrs Siddons? I'd as soon make love to the Archbishop of Canterbury!"

Horace Walpole had reservations about Mrs Siddons' acting. In a letter to the Upper Countess of Ossory he said,

I have visited and been visited by Mrs Siddons, and have seen and liked her much, yes very much in the passionate scenes in Percy, but I do not admire her in cool declamation, and find her voice very hollow and defective.

He also accused her of having "no originality" and made the curious remark, "when without motion her arms are not genteel." When Walpole asked Mrs Siddons, "in what part she would most wish me to see her? She named Portia in *The Merchant of Venice* but I begged to be excused."[16]

More than seven years had passed since Elizabeth first played Berinthia in *A Trip to Scarborough* but her performance was still fresh according to the Morning Chronicle of January 11th 1786. "We never saw anything more natually assumed or more agreeably wicked, if we may so phrase it, than the whole of Miss Farren's deportment in her scenes with Loveless."[17] Three days later she had a spectacular success when General Burgoyne's play, *The Heiress* written at Kowsley and dedicated to the Earl of Derby, was produced at Drury Lane. (General Burgoyne was Lord Derby's uncle by marriage having eloped with his father's sister, Lady Charlotte Stanley).

"The 14th was proudly distinguished by the production of *The Heiress* wrote Boaden. This was a highly successful comedy, based on Diderot's play, *Le Père de Famille*. In Boaden's view, Burgoyne was the only English writer to do justice to the genius of France. Gentleman Johnnie, as Burgoyne was called, said, "we must turn to France to find the graces of Apollo. Art, regularity, eloquence and delicacy; touches of sentiment, adapted only to the most polished manners, distinguish their theatre."

Praise came from all sides not only for the acting but for the play itself, Horne Tooke described it as, "the most perfect and meritorious comedy, without exception," and John Adolphus said it was, "the most effective novelty of the season . . . People of the highest fashion, the daily associates of the author, were pleased to see their manners represented with spirit and vivacity."[18]

Elizabeth played the heroine Lady Emily Gayville with great aplomb; Thomas King, stage-manager of Drury Lane was opposite her as Sir Clement Flint. She drew the comment that she "absolutely identified herself with this model of fashionable elegance".[19]

After praising the male actors Adolphus continued:-

> In the female characters, every actress shone . . . but above all, and to such a degree as to attract the separate thanks of the author, Miss Farren displayed her characteristic excellencies in Lady Emily Gayville. Where high and honourable sentiments, burning virtuous sensibility, sincere and uncontrollable affection, animated though sportive reprehension, elegant persiflage, or arch pointed satire, were the aim of the author, Miss Farren amply filled out his thought and by her exquisite representation made it, even when faint and feeble in itself, striking and forcible.

Add to these irresistible graces of her address and manner, the polished beauties of action and gait, and all the indescribable little charms which give fascination to the woman of birth and fashion, the power and inspiration of Miss Farren's performance may in some degree be appreciated. She had the feeling, judgement, grace and discretion.[20]

No actress of the day could ask for more.

Horace Walpole was enthusiastic about Elizabeth's acting and about the play too – he read it twice in one day. General Burgoyne's military career has no place here but referring later to his speeches as an MP, Walpole said that Burgoyne's battles and speeches would all be forgotten but his delicious comedy, *The Heiress* would still continue the delight of the stage and one of the most pleasing compositions. Burgoyne sold the copyright of *The Heiress* for £200. It went to ten editions in one year and was equally successful when translated into French, German, Italian and Spanish.

John Dowman's watercolour of Elizabeth and King in character was exhibited at the Royal Academy in 1787 and was so attractive that a demand for engravings set in. This was met by John Jones, and Frank Sabin's article in The Connoisseur described it as, "a very animated portrait of the Queen of Comedy, but the charm of the print is somewhat marred by the dwarfishness of her histrionic companion".

Below an engraving of a detail of the above portrait, appears this strange note.

There is in the portrait of the well-known actress a strong Semitic type; and I believe Elizabeth Farren had Jewish blood in her veins; as had also, to judge by Mrs Siddons' portrait, that other great actress.

Dowman gives no source for such an idea. There was no Jewish blood on the Farran side and if one goes by the appearance of her mother, none on that side either. Strangely, although Elizabeth's branch of the family separated from the ancestors of present day Farrans early in the eighteenth century, several of today's generation bear a remarkable resemblance to portraits of her.

The last comment here on Elizabeth in *The Heiress* comes from Mr William Ogilvie, second husband of Emily, Duchess of Leinster, who wrote to her in 1786 from London.

> ... been to the play ... seeing Nellie Farren in *The Heiress* and Mrs Jordan and was very pleased with both. I liked Miss Farren better than Mrs Abington; she is so uncommonly genteel, which the other never can attain with her vulgar fine airs.[21]

Did he know he was agreeing with Walpole?

Mr Ogilvie also provides evidence that Elizabeth was referred to as "Nellie", not short for Elizabeth as a rule but for "Ellen" or "Helen". Today, it could confuse her with the nineteenth century Music-Hall star, Nellie Farren, with whom there was no connection.

Anthony Pasquin, pseudonym for John Williams, wrote *The Children of Thespis* in 1786. This portrayed actors and actresses in verse. Elizabeth's section being over fifty lines, too long to quote in full. Here are the first fourteen lines.

> See Farren approach, whom Fates have design'd
> To fascinate hearts and illumine mankind ...
>
> See Pride kiss her sandals, and Apathy sighs
> And Honour implores, and Inconstancy dies.
>
> Her form is celestial; she looks friend between us
> A fourth lovely Grace or a sister of Venus;
> The mistress of Spring or the hand-maid of Flora
> To cheer human-kind like the rays of Aurora.
>
> As Taste shields her mind with the veil of refinement,
> And Cenius* expanded bursts forth from confinement;
> Great Jove views our Farren with rapturous wonder,
> Innerv'd by amazement, his hand drops the thunder ...
>
> Amid Beauty's children superior she shone,
> And Cupid's artillery plays round her zone ...[22]

There are only two references to parts in the poem; first to Lady

Teazle and in the second last line -

> But the slightest sweet Emmeline, that's her *chef d'oeuvre*.

Elizabeth's rise to fame on the stage and acceptance in High Society engendered envy in some who put the idea abroad that she would not have attracted attention but for the importance of her admirers, Fox and Lord Derby. But this was not so. The public, then as now, determines its theatrical favourites for itself, seeing and estimating their merits without any consideration of admirers. Given that it was not an asset in public eyes for an actress to be virtuous, no doubt Elizabeth's conduct attracted more comment than it would have done had her admirers been less in the limelight, but that is all. Whatever they wished people to believe, none could belittle Lord Derby's attention to Elizabeth. "The East wind has been as constant as Lord Derby"[23] wrote Horace Walpole to his friend Mary Berry after a particularly vicious spell of weather.

By the end of 1785, Elizabeth must have made arrangements with the Drury Lane management to have money in lieu of her benefit night. She gave a written receipt in April 1786 for, "One hundred and fifty Pounds in full for Benefit allowance for this season at Drury Lane Theatre."[24]

* Cenius (or Ceneus), son of Elatus and one of the Argonauts. Lampriere's Classical Dictionary 1827. p.81.

Chapter Five – Footnotes

1. Mathews, Mrs Chas. Anecdotes of Actors with other Desultory Recollections, 1864. p.1
2. Papendieck, op.cit. Vol.I. p.148
3. MacQueen Pope. Haymarket: Theatre of Perfection. 1948. p.134
4. Papendiek, op.cit. Vol.I. p.149
5. Ibid. p.149
6. Williams Wynn, Frances. Diary of a Lady of Quality. 1864. p.101
7. T.O.T., p.31
8. Boaden, Memoirs of Elizabeth Inchbald, 1833 p.71
9. Walpole, H. Letters of, ed. Mrs Paget Toynbee, 19 vols. 1903-25. Vol.13. No.2600.December 12th 1786
10. D.N.B.
11. Piozzi, Hester Lynch. (formerly Mrs. Thrale) Thraliana ed. Katherine Balderston, 1942. 17th June 1790. p.770
12. Piozzi, Hester Lynch. op.cit.
13. Mathews, Mrs. Tea Table Talk ,1824. p.42
14. The Public Advertiser, February 3rd 1785.
15. Papendiek, op.cit. Ch.6 p.95
16. Walpole to Countess of Uppper Ossory, January 15th 1788 From Powys, op.cit. p.327
17. Morning Chronicle, January 11th 1786.
18. Adolphus, op.cit. p.87
19. Colman, George the Younger. op.cit. Vol I, p.317
20. Adolphus, as n.17
21. Fitzgerald, Brian. Emily, Duchess of Leinster, 1950. p.178
22. Pasquin, Anthony. (Pseudonym) Children of Thespis ,1786.
23. Walpole, Letter to Mary Berry. 1791.
24. Elizabeth continued to have benefit nights outside London.

Chapter Six

The hey-day of the Richmond House plays came in 1787 and 1788 by which time private theatricals had become the most favourite diversion of the nobility and gentry. The rage would continue until about 1810. A craze for building private theatres had spread from France; there were several in London and others in the country. The Hon. Stephen Fox, son of Lord Holland and nephew of the Duke of Richmond had a "commodious theatre" next to his country seat, Winterslow House near Salisbury. Wynnstay, home of Sir Watkin Williams Wynn in Derbyshire, had the longest private theatricals which fell into two periods, 1770-1787 and 1803-1810. Here not only family and friends acted but if extras were needed the butler and other servants swelled the cast. These plays had a lasting effect on George Colman the Younger. His father hoped he would not follow a theatrical career but spending Christmas holidays at Wynnstay swayed him in that direction. No less a person than James Gandon, responsible for many of Dublin's architectural gems, designed the Wynnstay theatre.

In 1787 the plays at Richmond House were again supervised by Elizabeth. There was no theatre as such, plays were performed in rooms which had been converted by the most fashionable architect of the time, James Wyatt. Frederic Reynolds wrote, "After my return from Switzerland I found the whole town infected by another mania – Private Theatricals. Drury Lane and Covent Garden were almost forgotten in the performances at Richmond House." These were the amateur dramatics which aroused most envy and competition; they were also the most exclusive and fashionable in England while they lasted.

The private theatres had a reputation for enterprise in choice of plays, many adapted from the French. Experiments and innovations were made in lighting and the standard of scenery was high. Downman painted a series of portraits which included the half-length pastel of Elizabeth, now in the National Portrait Gallery, which was described as "full of piquancy and charm and exquisite in its mirroring of feminine archness and vivacity." It was exhibited at the Royal Academy in 1788 and Collyer's coloured engraving was in much demand. Mrs Damer's marble bust of Elizabeth as Thalia was also used on the Richmond House set.

Rehearsals for the first play in 1787, *The Way to Keep Him* by Arthur Murphy, started in February at the houses of General Conway and his daughter, the Hon. Mrs Damer.

Dramatis Personæ

Men

Mr Lovemore	The Earl of Derby
Sir Brilliant Fashion	The Hon.Richard Edgecumbe
William (servant to Mr Lovemore)	Sir Henry Englefield
Sideboard (servant to Sir Brilliant Fashion)	Mr Arabin

Women

Mrs Lovemore	The Hon. Mrs Damer
The Widow Belmore	The Hon. Mrs Hobart
Muslin (Maid to Mrs. Lovemore)	Mrs Bruce
Migionet (Maid to Mrs Belmore)	Mrs Blouse

On 18th April this report of a rehearsal before select friends, appeared in The Publick [sic] Advertiser.

Theatrical Intelligence

Last Thursday night, there was a *rehearsal* before some select friends to the amount of three-score, of the comedy *The Way to Keep Him;* the particulars of which we give on the authority of an honourable person who was present.

To compare this reproduction with the smoothness and mechanical uninterruption of common stage plays, it may be found somewhat deficient; but this we are warranted to say, that there were situations and points of expression in the acting, that would do credit to the most expert performers.

"Lord Derby was perfectly easy throughout, but gave specimen of great theatrical skill in those parts which he might very well be excused from knowing," ran one comment; "Lord Derby stands high in rank among noble Actors at Richmond House," another. Mrs Bruce, who played the maid Muslin, can hardly have been flattered by an aristocratic onlooker telling her, "My dear, if I did not know you to be a gentlewoman, I should swear you were born a chambermaid."

The Prologue by General Conway must have evoked earlier memories for Elizabeth.

> Since I was doomed to tread the awful stage
> Thank heaven that plac'd me in a polished age,
> There was a time, we're told, when in a cart
> I might have played this lovely Widow's part:
> Or travell'd like a Pedlar with a pack,
> And my whole homely wardrobe on my back ...

As the fourth line implies, the Prologue was spoken by Mrs Hobart. The Epilogue was written by Elizabeth's other friend, General Burgoyne and spoken by Mrs Damer. These are the opening lines.

> No Rainbow silks then flaunted in the wind;
> No Gauzes swell'd before; nor Cork behind.
> No Diamonds then with all their sparkling train,
> No, Rouge, nor Powder e'en a single grain ...

The Duke of Richmond limited the number in the audience and had an elaborate system of invitation/tickets which ensured it was also select. Arrangements were slightly different each time but the Duke reserved twenty tickets for himself, twelve for the Duchess and each actress, six for the writers of Prologue and Epilogue and one for Elizabeth as supervisor. With each invitation went the following:-

> The Duke and Duchess of Richmond present their compliments to Mr . . . and have the Honour of sending him His Ticket as a performer and four tickets at his Disposal for the Play of . . . for Thursday the . . . of . . . 178 . . . Mr. . . . is requested to insert in his own Hand Writing, on each Ticket the Name of the Person to be admitted, and to sign and seal it with his Arms. Mr . . . is also requested to send to Richmond House, on the Day before the Performance, a list of Persons for whom his Tickets are made out, without which they cannot be admitted.

It was taken for granted that all ticket holders had the right to bear arms and with such watertight arrangements, the Duke knew the names of everyone. The play began at 8 o'clock but everyone had to be seated by 7.30 p.m. The Prince of Wales was the one person whose friends were not checked as a newspaper announced, "The Prince of Wales has been furnished with a Ticket to admit himself and friends to the Private Theatre in Richmond House during three nights performances".

Select audiences at Richmond House were better behaved and quieter than those at public theatres where behaviour was anything but circumspect as described by a German visitor in 1791. After saying that the uproar before the play was "indescribable" he continued.

'. . . not only orange peels but sometimes glasses of water or other liquids were thrown from the gallery into the pit and boxes, so that frequently spectators are wounded and their clothing soiled. . . . one forgets one is in a playhouse which claims in its advertisements the title of a Royal Theatre. In Germany such disorder would never be tolerated even at a marionette show in a village inn. At Drury Lane I wished to look around the gallery in order to examine its structure, but a heap of orange peels, striking me with considerable force in the face, robbed me of all curiosity. The best plan is to keep your face turned to the stage, and thus quietly to submit to the hail of oranges on your back.'

Prompting was included in Elizabeth's duties during a Richmond House play; a seat adjoining the stage – called Farren's niche – was constructed for her but she never used it, preferring to stand throughout.

The importance of these private plays may be judged by a paragraph on April 20th, the day of the first performance of *The Way to Keep Him*, in the Morning Post.

> The amusements of this far-famed specimen of Aristocra-tick [sic] drama . . . an event not only of magnitude sufficient to interest the volatile taste of the great, but to suspend even more the serious movement of the political machine itself.

A debate in Parliament on the finances of the country, "is actually deferred until Monday, in consequence of the irresistible influence of this laudable offering to the shrine of the Dramatic Muse . . . this state of affairs cannot be acceptable to the readers of Morning Post".

Certainly priorities were peculiar for a little later a discussion of the Prince of Wales' affairs clashed with Richmond House and the latter had to give way.

The Gazeteer gave this general comment on Lord Derby's acting:

> Lord Derby in particular, displayed uncommon spirit, gaiety of deportment and thorough possession of the character" and "the performance throughout was uncommonly good; among the men Lord Derby was most particularly marked".
> The Theatre at Richmond House had everything to recommend it on Friday evening that elegance, beauty and expence [sic] could confer. The fine-toned voice of Lord

Derby, a voice which in a public theatre would excite a
roar of vociferous acclaimation [sic], would here receive
the tribute of a refined compliment . . .

The Duke of Richmond was said to be "looking into everything, the
superintendant and soul of the feast".

Not only the materials but the clothes were far in advance of those
in public theatres. The dresses worn by Mrs Damer were refined
models of decorum frequently suggested by herself and Mrs Siddons.
The latter had studied sculpture under Mrs Damer which influenced
her taste in clothes for the stage. Real jewellery was worn. "Mrs
Damer and Mrs Hobart were distinguished by a profusion of jewells
[sic] arranged with great elegance and effect."

The male actors were not to be outdone. "Lord Derby and Mr
Edgecumbe were most superbly habited . . ." Lord Derby had four
changes. "A chintz nightgown; a brown morning frock; a dauphin
colour embroidered with red and silver flowers and a very brilliant
star; a rich vest with a light brown coat." True to his part of Sir
Brilliant Fashion, Mr Edgecumbe wore richly embroidered crimson
velvet with quantities of rings, seals and diamond pins.

The final performance on May 17th brought the Richmond House
season to a close.

May 18th
Yes, even their Majesties and the Princesses, honoured the
Duke of Richmond with their presence at his Grace's
Theatre where the comedy of The Way to Keep Him was
performed by a select number of persons of fashion. The
Royal Family and their attendants were conveyed to
Richmond House in a train of seven carriages. Among the
Nobility and Gentry present on this occasion were the
Dukes of Chandos and Northumberland . . .

There followed a list of illustrious names and the paragraph
concluded,

Most of the foreign Ministers and a very brilliant assemblage of Ladies of the first beauty and accomplishments attended.

Exceptional arrangements were made for the King and Queen.

For the reception of their Majesties, a new box with a crimson canopy above, supported by pillars, richly gilt, on top a crown; the borders of the box were encircled in superb gold fringe.

The famous scene painter, Cornelius Dixon, had painted the apartment and there was a small box on each side for the princesses. No seats in the theatre were allowed to be occupied which would impede the view of their Majesties.

After the performance, there was a banquet and then a ball. "Their Majesties did not quit till after 1 o'clock in the morning; the Duke and Duchess Played Host and Hostess . . . which charmed every individual."

Among many favourable reports, the Countess of Upper Ossory struck a note of adverse criticism she had heard, in a letter to Horace Walpole who would have none of it. He suggested it emanated from a disappointed player and continued:-

who should act genteel comedy perfectly but people of fashion who have sense? Actors and actresses can only guess at the tone of high life, and cannot be inspired by it. Why are there so few genteel comedies but because most comedies are written by men not of that sphere? Etheridge, Congreve, Vanburgh and Cibber wrote genteel comedy because they lived in the best company; and Mrs Oldfield played it so well because she not only followed but often set the fashion. General Burgoyne has written the best modern comedy, for the same reason; Miss Farren is as excellent as Mrs Oldfield because she has lived with the best style of men in England.[1]

Horace Walpole was on his pet hobby-horse about the true representation of ladies and gentlemen on the stage being performed by those of good breeding. His remark about Elizabeth having "lived" with the best men must not be taken at face value. Mixed or consorted with would have been better. However he thought, erroneously, that Elizabeth was the exception which proved his rule, attributing her success in genteel comedy to the company she kept. He was evidently unaware that atavism had any hand in it, or that her breeding helped her rise to fame. As Dr W. J. Lawrence put it, "Blood may not tell as strongly on the stage as on the racecourse, but nevertheless it counts."[2]

Mrs Mathews opinion is apposite.

> To have merely mixed in genteel society will be insufficient to give a faithful portraiture of the higher class, – and, for the same reason that we apply to a fashionable tailor when we would have a fashionable coat – An initiation into the mysteries of polished manners is indispensable to a just resemblance of them.
>
> Our ordinary performers in representing *haut ton*, are apt to mistake and substitute *manner for manners:* they *affect* and *bon ton* has no affectation. It was Miss Farren's perfect intimacy with the better born that made her the accomplished woman of fashion she represented. There is much more simplicity in the personal manners of high life than most peoples acquainted with it imagine. Miss Farren *Par excellence* the *fine lady of her time* and she made Lady Teazle the same. She realised to her audience the grace and *bon ton* of existing manners.'[3]

Later on John Galt in retrospect considered Elizabeth's performances "marked with even more delight than Mrs Abington had been able to show in any of her performances; she presented a gentlewoman of the same nature, but in the opinion of the public, more refined."[4]

During the summer of 1787, Elizabeth had *The School for Scandal* for her benefit. The Duke and Duchess of Richmond, General Conway, the Hon. Mrs Damer and many other of her friends "showed their admiration and affection by their presence."

Over the years Elizabeth kept up a lively correspondence with her friends when they were out of London but during the summer of 1787, her letters to Sir Charles and Lady Dorothy Hotham were interrupted on account of her illness. Mrs Damer also corresponded with Sir Charles and frequently alluded to Elizabeth's delicate constitution saying it, "must occasion many anxious moments in those who know her, as it is scarcely possible to suppose them insensible to her merit and to the amiable qualities of her heart, setting aside her justly admired & superior talents". Here is part of her letter of August 21st (1787):

> . . . *Since I came to town I have been very uneasy about our dear Miss Farren, she has had terrible returns of the pain in her head has look'd so ill yr heart would have ached for her, I am sure; her doctor also forbids her writing, which is the reason that you have not heard from her at Dalton & it has caused her much anxiety I assure you. Today I promised to tell you this, for, tho' she plays tonight, she woud [sic] have written as she coud not bear deferring it any longer, but I was certain that you would have desired her not yourself. I think her better, & try to persuade her to give herself a little air & quiet, which woud [sic] recover her before the fatigue of the winter, I hope she will listen but you know how careless she is of her health. How I wished for you the night she played Beatrice: Her Glory was Great I assure you, a house full as it did hold, and very great applause — So great that I do not doubt that the play will be given again this winter* . . . [5]

Elizabeth did act Susan in *The Follies of the Day* on the night that letter was written and Lady Rustic in *The Country Attorney* on the following night, August 22nd, but she was evidently forced to take Mrs Damer's advice for according to the stage calendar, she did not act again until September 20th. During the interval, (her letter is undated), she wrote herself to Sir Charles.

> *Dear Sir Charles,*
> *I just write to say, I will write soon, but at present . . . my Head and hands are both full; ever since my return to town I have been under the direction of the Sons of Aesculapius; in plain English I have been so ill that I expected to take my departure for the other world: but thank Heaven I have now some hopes of staying a little longer in the Land of the living.*
> *I will write you a long letter soon, that will make you repent Ever having so tiresome a correspondent, in the meantime my best Love to kind Lady Dorothy and Miss Hotham. My Mother joins me in respects to all. And I remain Dear Sir Charles your very*
>
> > *Obliged and grateful*
> >
> > *Friend*
> >
> > *Eliza Farren*
>
> *Comp^ts. to Mr Kemble.*[6]

A little later, Kemble wrote to Sir Charles, "I am just come from my Lord Derby's, who is crippled by a bite from a goat." and at the same time Sir Charles had a letter from Mrs Damer which told him, "Goodwood is in a melancholy state just now, on account of poor Mr Ogilvie's accident, who was attacked by an elk, beat down, and so violently hurt that his life is in danger from the wounds and bruises this odious animal has given him."[7] (The owner of Goodwood, the Duke of Richmond, was Mr Ogilvie's brother-in-law).

After a lapse of six months the press announced, "The taste and Splendour of Richmond House are here again". Two comedies had been chosen to be performed in 1788.

The first was Mrs Centlivre's *The Wonder*. Under Elizabeth's guidance, rehearsals took place every night from December 18th, the plays having been read by the players during the previous ten days. Elizabeth must have worked them very hard as in just three weeks they were pronounced "almost word-perfect". The second play, *The Guardian* was adapted by Garrick from the French. There were new-comers amongst the actors; General Fitzpatrick, Lord John Townshend, William Ogilvie, Lord Henry Fitzgerald (fourth of Emily, Duchess of Leinster's seven sons). Her fifth son, Lord Edward Fitzgerald (who would die of wounds received while resisting arrest for high treason ten years later) also joined the actors at Richmond House but had to give up on account of illness.

During the rehearsals for the plays, there was another instance of their importance – Lord Gerald Fitzgerald, Emily, Duchess of Leinster's youngest son, was lost at sea in January. Although he was a nephew of the Duke of Richmond there was no interruption of rehearsals.

The Prince of Wales attended the first night of the plays, February 7th. The Dukes of York, Gloucester and Devonshire also came as well as Horace Walpole. It was only eight weeks after the first rehearsal and took place in the Duke's new theatre – the first time it had been used.

James Wyatt who had converted the rooms before, was responsible for its construction in the adjoining house on the left of Richmond House. The new seating was an innovation for the seats had backs, unlike public theatres at the period. Most of the scenery was this time painted by Thomas Greenwood, scene painter at Drury Lane, but Lord Henry Fitzgerald did "a sketch for the Design of The Terriero de Passo . . . who in his Tour, passed some time in Spain".

Lord Henry was an asset to Richmond House; a born actor with much experience in tragedy in amateur dramatics in Ireland though comedy was new to him. His Don Felix in *The Wonder* was judged to be as good as that of the late David Garrick and unlike the latter, he had the height and figure for it. Horace Walpole wrote that he was "amazed. Lord Henry is a prodigy, a perfection – all passion, nature and ease; . . . Garrick was a monkey to him in Don Felix, then he is so much the man of fashion and so genteel. In short when people of quality can act, they must act their own parts so much better than others can mimic them". Walpole's hobby-horse again.

Lord Henry began to rival Lord Derby as an actor. Mrs Siddons did not endear herself to the Duchess of Leinster or her family by expressing her opinion that Lord Derby was by far the better of the two.

Lord Henry's artistic bent was used in arranging the men's clothes in *The Wonder*. They were all in Spanish style which answered well, the play being set in Portugal. He himself was resplendent in "a white satin vest and breeches with crimson slashes decorated with gold lace and with a richly embroidered cloak of crimson velvet; a blaze of diamonds shone from his hat." Hoppner's portrait of him as Don Felix was exhibited at the Royal Academy the next year, 1789, immortalising his success as an actor.

Seven performances of the bill were played and the King and Queen saw it on March lst. At that time, Lord Henry Fitzgerald was acting the part of Don Pedro. The papers said "the Great Theatric business going on is the subject of all fashionable conversation; once again Lord Henry Fitzgerald and Lord Derby were very excellent."

Two more plays were acted at Richmond House in the next bill; *The Jealous Wife*, by George Colman the Elder, and a tragedy called *Theodosius*, in which Lord Henry's acting of the death scene was so convincing that two ladies were carried out in a faint!

The last play acted at Richmond House for all time was *False Appearances*, adapted by Elizabeth's friend, Henry Seymour Conway, (now a Field Marshal) from *Les Dehors Trompeurs* by Louis De Boissy. It was in that play – in French – that the Duke of Richmond, then Lord March, had had his first taste of private theatricals at the age

91

of five.

Mrs Lybbe Powys was at the first night on May 23rd and wrote, 'The Prologue and epilogue were both very clever; wrote by General Conway, and spoken with great spirit by Lord Derby and Mrs Damer. The whole was amazingly well acted. The house was filled with all the fine people in town.'[8]

Lord Henry was praised again and Lord Derby singled out for his by-play and crispness of dialogue. Behind all the discussion and praise, Elizabeth was the hub of the wheel, working hard and willingly to give of her knowledge and expertise and she gets a mention, "the brilliancy of the audience was scarcely to be parallelled, and much praise is due to Miss Farren under whose management the whole was conducted. After the play was concluded the company was entertained to supper, which consisted of a variety of covers, and a dessert in the first style of elegance."

It was anxious work shouldering the responsibility of the whole production which evidently took its toll as Mrs Damer wrote to Sir Charles Hotham after *False Appearances*:-

> *I cannot express, yet I do firmly believe that our dear Miss Farren suffered still more, I shall never forget the anxiety of her fine expressive countenance which I only saw at a distance, for she would not venture near us till the Play was over.*[9]

The next year *False Appearances* was acted at Drury Lane. Elizabeth's letter to Sir Charles Hotham mentions it:

> *Vous avez tort mon cher Ami and I coud find it in my Heart to be very angry with you for daring to think that Mrs Damer loves you more than I do; the truth is, you love her better than you do me & therefore you fancy that she ought to return your passion with a greater degree of warmth. Own that I am right; you are at a great distance you know & therefore*

need not have fear of **Nails** before your Eyes, besides I will let you into a little Secret, the Lady in question has so many good qualities that I should have a bad Opinion of your taste if your Love did not increase in proportion to her Merit. You see I am content to come off **second best** upon this occasion; a proof at least that vanity is not among the greatest of my failings.

I know not whether you are blessed with such weather in Yorkshire as we Enjoy in Town? but of all the burning fiery furnaces since **Shadrack, Meshack & Abed-nego** nothing ever equalld [sic] the heat of my room at this Moment, not a breath of air and I am ashamed to mention the dress I am writing to you in tho' I am sure your goodness woud excuse it, shocking as the word **Chemise** must be to a delicate ear. Heavens! I have let it escape my Pen! tant pis; you must not read it to Ly Dorothy. We are very profligate in this wicked Town, but I see no reason why we should make you **Country folks** as bad as ourselves!

Laying all this nonsense aside, I must tell you My Dear Sir Charles how much, how very much we miss you here; our pleasant Party seems all quite deranged, & we never meet but a sigh escapes each of us for the loss of our Charming friends in Yorkshire; this is not a way of speaking but literally true.

On Saturday we bring out "Les Dehors-Trompeurs"; you will not wonder that I am extremely anxious for its success, as you know how much General Conway & all the family are interested in it; I shall, with regret, to the forsaken Corner "where civil Speech & Soft Persuasion hung", turn many a wistful look, but all in vain, no friendly hand will be held out with **"I'm glad your Come"**, no soft little Voice will issue below with "**Come, Come Down here, I have kept you a place**", – upon my Word, 'tis quite *melancholy to think of it, for, after all, 'tis these little offices kindly done that renders Life desirable, or indeed worth the keeping; if people did but [sic] know how giving & receiving little **Douceurs** betters **Life** they woud study the Agreable [sic] from Mere Motives of Selfishness; I know you will agree with me.*

I shall not say anything of Drury Lane, as you will have better intelligence from two quarters & no other news have we . . .

By this time I take it you are pretty well tired of me, and will thank me for making my Congé. Adieu, then my Estimable friend, if you find me a tedious & prolix Correspondent, you must thank yourself, "O'er strained indulgence Spoils the forward Child."

May all happiness attend you

Ever Sincerely Yours

Eliza Farren
From Ld Derby, first to her Ladyship Everything that is tender, then to you Everything friendly, myself to both Ladies Love & Gratitude.[10]

A valuable letter for its insight into Elizabeth's character and feelings. The date *False Appearances* was produced at Drury Lane was April 20th, 1789, and General Conway paid Elizabeth the compliment of dedicating it to her with thanks for "advice and patronage you favoured it with as a friend on its appearance in its first form at Richmond House". It was only a moderate success, lacking the glitter and splendour of its first venue.

On October 5th 1788, Mrs Damer wrote to Sir Charles Hotham.

. . . Now for the Play, alas! alas! The Duke of Richmond wrote me word when I was at Spa that he meant to give

up his Theatre, that he found it troublesome & wanted
the House for other purposes, yet if I wished it very much
he wou'd continue it one year more. I coud make but one
answer to this, which I am sure I need not tell you; & I
gave up the most agreeable amusement as lost. I disliked
this so much that, as ill news flys [sic] fast enough, I
scarce mentioned it to anyone. Since I came to England I
have seen the Duke, he did not mention the subject to me,
& I of course did not chuse (sic) to begin it, yet I hear the
poor dear Theatre still exists - this is all I know.[11]

Not long afterwards, the new theatre at Richmond House was
adapted to accommodate a relative of the Duke, Colonel Charles
Lennox and his wife Lady Charlotte. Richmond House was destroyed
by fire just before Christmas 1791. The blaze began at 8 am, upstairs,
so many valuables were saved, the Duke assisting himself until noon.
When the flames were at their height, the Duke saw to his horror,
his favourite spaniel panic-stricken at an upstairs window. The
flames were licking the panes and the Duke offered a reward to any
rescuer. Ladders were lashed together and the dog brought down; the
rescuer received eleven gold guineas and the man who held the
ladder, three guineas.

Richmond House was never rebuilt. Later the Duke supervised the
building of a theatre at Chichester, near his Sussex estate of
Goodwood. He gave much of the beautifully painted scenery from
the private theatre in Privy Gardens, Whitehall.

It was during the Richmond House season that an amusing incident
occurred involving Lord Derby. Although he and Elizabeth were
considered as engaged, one night behind the scenes at Richmond
House, Lord Derby acted out a formal proposal of marriage to
Elizabeth. He must have cut a funny figure in his quaint theatrical
clothes with his stage make-up for dress rehearsal.[12]

After the closure of the Richmond House theatre and during the
Drury Lane recess, Elizabeth went to stay at Park Place with Lady

Ailesbury. Her daughter, Mrs Damer wrote to Sir Charles. "Miss Farren has passed some days with us here & lookd in most remarkable beauty, so that you must, if this continues, turn your shield towards that part of your heart most vulnerable to her eyes." After her visit to Park Place, Elizabeth wrote to Lady Dorothy Hotham.

> *My Dear Lady Dorothy,*
> *You are married to the falsest Man; you never will believe that he goes about seeking whom he may devour, and deceiving young Virgins into a kindness for him! but I have found him out, and give him up. And now, my dear Friend, I must tell you that I am just come to town from Park Place, where I have been a great while, and where we often wishd for you & that* **saucy Man** *belonging to you. All your* **Dears** *are in good health and Spirits.*
> *Your Ladyship I doubt not is much pleased with the New Manager of Drury Lane [Kemble], and to say* **truth** *to you, he goes the way to please everybody; he uses me* **very ill** *tho', I must tell you, for he* **coaxes me** *to do all sorts of things.*
> *General Burgoyne is this Moment coming up the Street with Mr Jephson, who he has beggd [sic] to present to me, I must therefore bid you adieu, first assuring you that I am with respects and affection your*
> *Ladyship's obliged and grateful*
> *Eliza Farren*
>
> *Mama sends her respects to Sir Charles and your Ladyship. Do not give* **my** *love to the Creature.*[13]

This is Elizabeth's only reference to her virginity.

Chapter Six – Footnotes

All information regarding the Richmond House Theatre taken from Charles Burney's Theatrical Register, 1777-1797, British Museum Reference Library.

1. Walpole, Toynbee. op.cit. No. 2612
2. Lawrence, Dr W.J., op.cit. p.95
3. Mathews, Mrs, Tea Table Talk p.44
4. Galt. op.cit. p.230
5. Hotham MSS. Deposited Brynmor Jones Library, University of Hull and reproduced by kind permission of the Hull University Archivist.
6. Ibid
7. Ibid
8. Powys, Caroline. op.cit. p.300 (see note 21)
9. Hotham MSS
10. Ibid
11. Ibid
12. Baron-Wilson, Mrs Cornwell, Memoirs of Harriot, Duchess of St Albans. 1839 p.186
13. Hotham MSS

Chapter Seven

Side by side with her private activities and social life, Elizabeth's public performances continued – during rehearsals of the *Bon Ton* theatricals she was acting three or four nights a week – often in a different play each night as well as in the after piece. Houses were packed and box-office receipts high. Enthusiasm for her acting brought not only her admirers and friends but foreign visitors to the theatre. One Swiss said she was "tall and perfectly graceful; her face was beautiful and expressive". Another, Henri Meister – his mother was French and he inclined to that country in taste – had this to say.

> The English Stage can at present boast of possessing Comic performers of extraordinary excellence; such are Miss Farren and Mrs Jordan. The former has great taste and elegance in appearance, if you except the custom with women in this country, which is that of pressing their elbows too closely behind them. She has the most lovely countenance, appears to be full of vivacity and spirit and hits off the air of a woman of fashion exactly. It is said that Lord Derby only waits for the moment he shall be at liberty to offer her his hand. There is no circle wherin [sic] her ladyship, as she will then be styled, need fear finding herself out of her sphere. Her tone of voice has naturally something of dryness and sharpness in it, but she moderates these defects by the most correct and the exactest pronunciation. There is sometimes too much art and stiffness perceptible in her manner of acting. These faults are amply made up by just and accurate conception of her character, and a chaste and lively *performance* of it! She is

particularly admirable in *The School for Scandal*, in the character of Lady Emily in *The Heiress*, and in *The Wives Confederacy*. What will make you downright in love with her, is, that they tell me, she is as declared a democrat as the noble lord her sweetheart! Mrs Jordan's style of acting is not so extensive and is adapted to a smaller number of characters; yet some parts are more striking and natural. Her figure is neither so genteel or so sprightly as Miss Farren's[1]

Given that the national character is always revealed in the playhouses, Meister considered *The School for Scandal* and *The Heiress* presented, "the most faithful and vivid picture of present-day manners," having, "all the wit, all the vitality of ancient comedy, at least as much of both as is compatible with the decency of the characters . . ." He ends the passage with a good word for Mrs Jordan who was less versatile than Elizabeth but, "her charm more simple, more naive, and the gaiety of her acting fresher and more contagious."[2]

Another German commentator wrote of Sheridan's *The Rivals* as being a great comedy, "Sparkling with wit . . . the hero Faulkland admirably drawn and his Julia has a femininity that is now rare on the English stage. Miss Farren played Julia quite well . . ." He goes on to say that in high comedy, Elizabeth cannot match up to Mrs Abington and concludes, "Miss Farren is given more admiration than she deserves, a fault which all theatre audiences in all countries have in common at present."[3]

Boaden was not an admirer of Mrs Jordan in genteel comedy saying that "she could not assume the high tone of manners characteristic of elegant comedy; the fashionable woman of Mrs Jordan always had some *tang* of the country girl. . . . It was a smart soubriette who hurried on her ladyship's clothing and *overacted* the character to avoid being detected." Neither could she cope with anything serious as he added, "her tragedy too was insufferable."[4]

Elizabeth's sister Margaret (Peggy) had become a competent actress but there is little about her until Tate Wilkinson tells that she had been to Scotland and Ireland in 1786 and returned to his company "greatly improved indeed"; he gave her a fixed engagement. She was said to resemble Elizabeth in appearance but not in character being accused of a malign wit and she is never mentioned in the social scene. She became engaged to an actor in Wilkinson's company, Thomas Knight, and in 1787, Colman gave Elizabeth permission to tour the Northern Circuit and to act in her sister's farewell benefit before her marriage to Mr Knight. This was at Leeds on July 20th 1787. Peggy herself played "the Poor Soldier and stood her ground so well, that it proved a strong card for her".[5]

Elizabeth played Lady Paragon in *The Natural Son* and her reception was so enthusiastic that she got Colman's permission to return to Leeds for July 30th, August 1st and 2nd after she had been to York.

It was Assize week in York and "By Desire of the High Sheriff and the Gentlemen of the Grand Jury", she played Lady Teazle in *The School for Scandal* and Emmeline in *King Arthur* for her benefit night on July 28th. "Miss Farren drew great houses, attended with every respect, admiration and attention She could possibly expect, or her infinite merit deserve," wrote Tate Wilkinson. "She obtained and rivetted the affections and esteem of all."

Her return visit to Leeds was hugely successful and Tate Wilkinson wrote with regret that he "wished her a good journey to the metropolis and thanking her for her good services, her bewitching company, and her agreeable everything, will imagine she is safely arrived at her snug house in Green Street, London".[6]

During the summer recess of 1787, Drury Lane was again refurbished as John Philip Kemble recounted to Sir Charles Hotham.

> You will be highly gratified I am sure when you see with what Elegance our Theatre is refitted . . . I speak serious Truth; though I must think the House ought in Justice to be

seen, before the smoaky [sic] Lamps have dull'd the Gold and darken'd the White, and wither'd the Bloom of the rose-coloured Linings to the Boxes . . .[7]

The letter is dated September 19th, so the theatre was just about to open for the 1787/88 season.

August 1789 saw Elizabeth back in York for race-week, "this Royal week, this joyful week", as Tate Wilkinson called it.[8] Much of society was there and flocked to the theatre. Elizabeth opened on the Monday night as Beatrice in *Much Ado About Nothing*. Walpole and Mary Berry agreed that it was not one of her best parts but the Prince of Wales and the Duke of York saw it that night and took such a penchant for Elizabeth, that the public were greatly influenced and on COMMAND night, "a sum not often received at any theatre in Great Britain, out of London" was taken – £197.10s. Tate Wilkinson gave the following account of Elizabeth's week in York.

Miss Farren played the Royal week, 4 nights at York, and was in high esteem, not only as an elegant and beautiful woman, but as a charming actress, who received not only plaudits on the stage, but applause more lasting by a discerning list of persons of the first rank of both sexes, who daily paid their respects at the shrine, not only of attraction but of *Goodness* – What can be more properly attractive? As in Miss Farren we behold not only a virtuous, amiable, and sensible woman, but that splendour of private worth, made still more valuable by her chiefest pleasure and attention being employed in fulfilling the duties of a child, to render her mother's life truly happy. Such is the picture of true worth.[9]

In case Elizabeth is in danger of being thought a stuffy goody-goody, it is worth remembering she was called "the merry Irish girl" who retained and restrained the affection of Lord Derby. The same source says, "the merry Miss Farren, whose beauty, wit and vivacity won

101

all hearts."[10]

Tate Wilkinson followed the curious custom of the day, comparing two actresses in a scale of merit – even though one of them was long dead.

Scale of Merit

Mrs Woffington tall	So is Miss Farren
Mrs Woffington beautiful	So is Miss Farren
Mrs Woffington elegant	So is Miss Farren
Mrs Woffington well-bred?	So is Miss Farren
Mrs Woffington had a harsh and discordant voice.	Miss Farren's voice is musical and bewitching.
Mrs Woffington could be rude and vulgar.	Miss Farren *never*.[11]

Tate Wilkinson continued, 'I can compliment the present age on their possessing an actress, in a first and polished character, the arch and attractive Miss Farren. Such parts as Lady Townley, Maria, Millamant etc. now represented by her, were formerly thought Mrs Woffington's best line of acting. Miss Farren is certainly very like Peg Woffington in some points, and enchantingly superior in others; Miss Farren, as to every intrinsic quality, may bid the world look on, scrutinize and envy. . . . So undoubtedly Miss Farren seizes the wreath of Fame with security as she adds to her perfection in the Scale of Merit, virtue, modesty, reverence for a parent and every other endearing quality: therefore with propriety and for the credit of the Drama, let me hurl my cap in the air and cry – Long Live The Farren.'[12]

Wilkinson doesn't mention that Elizabeth could not hold a candle to

Peg Woffington's able and high-spirited handling of breeches parts. Her many promiscuous affairs were common knowledge and she played male parts so well and so often that one day, after acting Sir Harry Wildair in *The Constant Couple*, she said to the actor Quin, 'I have played this part so often that half the town believe me to be a man,' to which Quin replied, 'Madam, the other half *knows* you to be a woman'.

In the theatre Elizabeth was friendly with all her colleagues, not at all arrogant or superior but she kept her distance and made no close friends except Mrs Siddons and Mrs Inchbald of whom her mother approved. Mrs Abington and the others bore her no ill-will on this account, indeed Mrs Abington must have had a generous and appreciative nature for watching Elizabeth, "the applause of that lady was praised as a mark of becoming liberality in a great genius, above such a pitiful feeling as jealousy."[13] Mrs Siddons was different. "It is strenuously asserted that Mrs Siddons never did applaud any actress upon the stage."[14]

Mrs Inchbald observed, "To have fixed degrees and shades of female virtue, possessed at this time by the actresses of The Haymarket Theatre, would have been employment for an able casuist." Then she told this story.

> One evening, about half an hour before the curtain was drawn up, some accident happened in the dressing-room of one of the actresses, a woman of known intrigue, she ran in haste to the dressing-room of Mrs Wells, to finish her toilet. Mrs Wells, who was mistress of the well-known Captain Topham, shocked at the intrusion of a reprobated woman, who had a worse character than herself, quitted her own room and ran to Miss Farren's crying, 'What would Captain Topham say, if I were to remain in such company?' No sooner had she entered the room, to which as asylum she had fled, than Miss Farren flew out of the door repeating, 'What would Lord Derby say, if I should be seen

103

in such company?'[15]

Elizabeth's mother had a point in advising her to choose her theatrical friends carefully!

Amongst her close friends Elizabeth numbered Mrs Piozzi, formerly Mrs Thrale and at that time a great friend of Dr Johnson's. Under the date 11th March 1789, Mrs Piozzi writes, "Miss Farren is now all that Man desires in Woman I believe".[16] Further on is a poem she had written in Italian about Elizabeth. Here is her English translation.

1

In that Roguish Face one sees
All her Sex's Witcheries;
Playful Sweetness, cold Distain
Everything to turn one's Brain.

2

Sparkling from Expressive Eyes
Heaving in affected sighs,
Sure Destruction still we find,
Still we lose our Peace of Mind

3

Touch'd by her half trembling hand
Can the coldest heart withstand?
While we dread the starting Tear
And the tender accents hear.

4

Numberless are sure the Ways
That she fascinates our Gaze
Magic lists her Pow'r improve,
Witcheries that wait on Love.[17]

John Philip Kemble took over as manager of Drury Lane on September 22nd 1788 and his sister, Mrs Siddons, wrote that day to Sir Charles Hotham, "I am ready to burst . . . God knows how he will be able to go through such a fag as it will be".

Already in a letter to Lady Dorothy, Elizabeth had made it clear she was none too pleased by the appointment. She had a sharp temper and clashed with Kemble on several known occasions.

All through his years at Drury Lane, Kemble kept meticulous journals giving details of receipts, plays and the acting. His first mention of Elizabeth was on December 17th, "Great Quarrel with Miss Farren about her Dress; she acted at last, however, for I wd not change the Play for her Humour". *(The Suspicious Husband)*.[18] Just before taking over at Drury Lane Kemble had written to Sir Charles Hotham, "I have not seen Miss Farren since I came to Town, and the only Refuge I can find from the Tempest of her Displeasure is to be afraid that she does not care whether I see her or not". No love lost between them it seems.

Kemble had trouble with Mrs Jordan too who, on December 21st, 'fancied herself ill. I spent about two Hours in coaxing her to act. N.B. she was as well as ever She was in her Life, and stayed when she was done her Part to see the whole Pantomime'.[19]

Later he says, "Mrs Jordan, confesses herself well, but won't appear in any Play with Miss Farren".[20] This obtained for several years.

Bewailing the weather, Kemble made this entry on January 1st 1789, "I am very sorry my luck was to commence Manager this year. The Theatre laboured under great Disadvantages from the frequent Indispositions of the Performers, from the uncommon severity of the winter . . ." (Elizabeth did not appear between Tuesday 13th and Friday 23rd) and Kemble added, "His Majesty's Indisposition also affected audiences".[21]

Later that year, in June 1789, Elizabeth and her mother went to Dublin. Although there is no corroboration for her acting there in 1779, she had appeared at Crow Street Theatre in 1784. She and her mother had kept in touch with her father's first cousin, Charles Farran of the Court of the Exchequer in Dublin and probably stayed with him in 1784. His town house in York Street, an elegant street of fine houses running westward from Stephen's Green, was within walking distance of the theatre. These houses had handsome hall-doors of differing design, each surmounted by an artistic fanlight serving the dual purpose of lighting a dark hall-passage and deterring thieves by the decorative iron grille. Most of the houses have been demolished though a row of facades remains, which has new buildings behind it. It was in 1784 that Elizabeth met her second cousin Charles Farran junior, (fifteen at the time), with whom she struck up a life-long friendship.

In 1789, the journey to Dublin was long, uncomfortable and often hazardous. First by stage-coach for several days to the chosen port where the wait could be long – no steam-boats so one had to delay until the weather and particularly the wind, was favourable enough to sail across the sea. The duration of the voyage was entirely at the mercy of the elements and depended from what quarter the wind blew and its strength. It was exceedingly uncomfortable in the boat which was filled to capacity with passengers, crew and horses packed closely and the journey was fraught with danger, Dublin Bay being littered with wrecks from numerous fatalities.

John O'Keefe, the Irish actor and playwright – described by Hazlitt as the English Molière – only crossed the sea five times. One of these journeys which had begun in Liverpool (where he was wind-bound for a week), the wind changed after embarkation and the boat was tossed about for five nights. The distraught passengers implored the captain to put them ashore "anywhere at all" and eventually he did so, at Holyhead. There O'Keefe waited another week – three in all – before he could begin again.

Dublin was the second city in His Britannic Majesty's dominions and ranked with the finest in Europe for extent, magnificence and commerce. Handsome buildings such as Trinity College and the Royal Hospital, Kilmainham – a gem by any standards – had already been joined by some fine squares and terraces of private houses. Of the fine mansions, Leinster House, built by Cassels in 1745 for the Earl of Kildare (later 1st Duke of Leinster) in the country district of Molesworth Fields, set the fashion for living on the south side of the city. Said to be the prototype of the White House in Washington, it is now the Irish Parliament (the Dail). Elizabeth's sponsor, Emily, Duchess of Leinster was its first hostess.

Charles Farran also bought an estate on the south side of Dublin; this was called Rathgar – now the name of a sprawling suburb – but then a very isolated spot.

The Irish nobility and gentry favoured Stephen's Green for town houses. Mrs Delany wrote, "I think it may be preferred justly to any square in London" (Elizabeth's second cousin, John Farran, lived in No.6). She said too that Dublin exhibited "great Sociableness"; Lord Cloncurry wrote, "It was one of the most agreeable places of residence in Europe . . . society in the Upper classes was as brilliant and polished as that of Paris in its best days, while social intercourse was conducted with a conviviality that could not be equalled in France".[23] Earlier in the century – and it had not changed – Horace Walpole observed, "Ireland which one did not suspect is become the staple of wit, and I find coins bon-mots for our greatest men", and A.J. Froude found that Dublin not only had a flourishing intellectual life but that besides her orators, Ireland produced artists, men of letters, statesmen, soldiers, the best of which the Empire could boast.

Richard Cumberland pointed out, "the professions were more intermixt [sic] and ranks more blended," which made for very lively discourse which was especially so when members of the legal profession were present for they were the most elegant and witty of all. (Four of Elizabeth's Farran cousins were Dublin lawyers). There was a general spirit of conviviality.

The liveliness of the scene was no doubt assisted by the vast quantity of wine that was drunk, particularly claret which was often served from huge silver flagons. Contrasting drinking habits of the time, Bishop Berkeley said that English gentlemen with incomes of £1,000 a year often did not provide wine for guests but those on £100 a year in Ireland did so. Lord Chesterfield when he was viceroy, deplored the excessive drinking and once expressed the hope "that God would turn all their wine sour".

According to Arthur Young, "Claret is the common wine of all tables and so much inferior to what is drunk in England that it does not appear to be the same wine." He added that the Port in Ireland was incomparable.

As for the theatre, Walker's Hibernian Magazine pointed out, "an attention to the theatre will indicate the good taste of the age, as neglect of it will manifest the contrary". Dublin has always been a centre for good theatre and it was lively and flourishing in 1789. Private theatricals were as popular in Ireland as in England and the Duke of Leinster's house, Carton, Co. Kildare, was an early venue for amateurs.

Reference to her journey to Ireland in 1789 comes in Elizabeth's letter to Sir Charles Hotham; it is undated but must have been early in the summer recess.

> *My Good Dear Sir Charles,*
>
> *I have but time for a line to return my warmest thanks for your kind Letter, and to assure you of my safe arrival at this Place, after a Journey & Voyage more tiresome than I can express.*
>
> *I have been received here in such a way that if I was to live a thousand Years I cou'd never forget; all Dublin I believe have been to see me, & I have literally hardly time to turn Myself. They are Charming People and I can never be half grateful enough for their attention to me.*
>
> *The Duchess of Leinster (with whom I live, almost) desires me to say every thing kind to Ly Dorothy & yourself. My Mother joins me in most affectionate respects to her Ladyship, and I remain, dear Sir Charles*

Most truly obliged & affecte Friend

Eliza Farren.

> *I have a message from Ld Henry to her Ladyship, but must not tell you.*[24]

More first hand news of Elizabeth in Dublin comes from Mrs Damer who quotes Mr Ogilvie, Elizabeth's host.

> ... Of our friends I have to tell you that I hear the most pleasing accounts from Ireland of Miss Farren that can be wished, the first & second night over, the most brilliant audience & every mark of applause. Mr Ogilvie was so obliging, of himself, as to write to me this satisfactory intelligence & that of her being received with open arms & as she deserves so well by the Duchess of Leinster & many other Ladies who shew her every possible attention. I have heard also from herself &, as far as I can judge thro' the hurry in which she writes, I flatter myself that her journey will answer in every respect, as you and I thought it wou'd.[25]

The Dublin Evening Post wrote of "the peculiar excellency of her dramatical performances," and concluded "public humanity, gratefully pays her tribute due to her generous farewel [sic] of a Dublin audience – a free performance for confined Debtors".[26]

The manager of the theatre had stipulated with Elizabeth, "play or pay £500"; that was her stipend for the trip and would have been her forfeiture if she had not come. In the event she carried away a thousand pounds and the manager made the same amount of profit.

Mrs Siddons wrote to Sir Charles a month later, on August 30th.

> ... Yorkshire is now extremely gay, I suppose. The gay & lovely Miss Farren has been, perhaps is now with you. I am very glad to hear of her success in Ireland, & beg to trouble you with my Comp[ts] to her, if I could envy her

anything, it would be the pleasurable days she spends with you & dear Lady D . . . [27] .

Mrs Siddons may not have applauded any actress in the theatre but she was not grudging of her praise on paper.

The 1789/1790 season at Drury Lane was due to start on September 16th but no firm arrangements had been made with Elizabeth by 15th when Kemble wrote that day in his Journal:-

I waited upon Miss Farren in the Evening in Consequence of her having sent me word that she would not act The Heiress next Day. The Revd Mr E . . . went with me. She told me her Engagement was not Settled, and that she would not perform unless her Salary were encreased [sic] from eighteen to twenty Pounds a week. I informed her that I could not take the Liberty of raising her Salary without Mr Sheridan's Consent, that he was out of Town, that I would let him know her Demands immediately and in the mean-time hoped she wld not distress the Affairs of the Theatre by refusing to Act the next night – After two hours Entreaty she consented to perform the ensuing Evening . . . [28]

Sheridan assured Kemble that he had met Elizabeth one day in the Spring at Mr Hammersley's Bank when she reminded him that her engagement had not been renewed. He had said that was because of "hurry of Business but hoped we should have the Pleasure of her Company at the opening of the Season nevertheless; she replyed [sic], certainly if he wished it, that she was quite Contented with her old Conditions . . ." The truth of the matter is not known but Sheridan had such a bad name for paying at all, let alone raising any salary, it makes one wonder. He told Kemble, "though I freely give her Leave to choose her own Dresses which was a Point she seemed in her Conversation with me to have much at Heart, yet pray tell her I cannot agree to encreasing [sic] her Salary". Sheridan told Kemble then, he had lately added £100 a year to Elizabeth's income as without it she could not "afford herself a carriage".[29]

Kemble may have been apprehensive of conveying all this to Elizabeth but she only answered that if she could not have her wish, she could not, that she was not the person to squabble for a pound or two a week, "but Mr Sheridan would sometime be sorry for his refusal". (Her salary remained at £18 until her retirement eight years later). There are no more references to the contretemps but Elizabeth did *not* act in *The Heiress* on September 16th; she did not appear at Drury Lane at all until September 26th. That night she did act Lady Emily Gayville in *The Heiress*. Presumably Kemble had to manage without her for the first ten days of the new season.

In spite of difficulties with Elizabeth, Kemble greatly admired her acting and after her performance as Lady Bell in Murphy's *Know Your Own Mind* on October 10th, he wrote that it was, "very fine", while three days later her acting of Dorinda in his version of *The Tempest* drew this comment:-

13th October *The Tempest* rec'd with great applause – Miss
Farren and Mrs Moody acted inimitably.

He was enthusiastic about General Burgoyne's Epilogue which gave a "fine close" to the play spoken by "the Enchanting Farren". Here it is:

One, who on station scorns to found controul [sic]
But gains pre-eminence by worth of Soul.
These are the honours that, on Reason's plan,
Adorn the Prince, and vindicate the Man;
While gayer passions, warm'd at Nature's Breast,
Play o'er his youth – the feathers of his crest.

The Prince of Wales had been in the audience and after Elizabeth had spoken the Epilogue an onlooker wrote, "I would offer the last couplet triumphantly, as an attestation to the refined genius of Burgoyne. The mixed tone of tenderness, airiness and respect, with which Miss Farren delivered the last line, can never be forgotten".

"Play o'er his YOUTH – the feathers of his crest"

Elizabeth repeated Dorinda in *The Tempest* – and spoke the Epilogue – on many occasions but no comment ever surpassed that after the performance of November 3rd.

> Miss Farren is almost beyond criticism; she is always animated, hurries you away, and does not leave you time to reflect. We are not too bold in asserting that Europe does not produce a finer actress in these lively, natural characters.[30]

Moving around in fashionable society, Lord Derby and Elizabeth continued to attract comment, spoken and written on account of the platonic nature of their association but even the arch-gossip James Boswell, had nothing disagreeable to say. Here is an entry in his Journal on December 24th 1789.

> Dined at Kemble's with Malone, Courtenay and son, Murphy and Sir Joshua Reynolds. Mrs Kemble was very pleasing. At coffee and tea were Miss Farren and her Mother and Lord Derby. I was quite delighted with the english [sic] accent of Mrs Kemble and Miss Farren. I did not drink much wine. I felt myself not quite expert in easy chat, but exulted in the difference between this society and any in Scotland. Lord Derby was very pleasant. The attachment between him and Miss Farran was, I really thought, as fine a thing as I had ever seen: truly virtuous admiration on his part, respect on hers.[31]

Murphy, the Irish playwright was a close friend of Dr Johnson's; he refers to him as, "dear Mur".

On the crest of her success Elizabeth had some power over Kemble. He wrote on October 25th 1789, "This was the first night of *The False Friend* altered from Sir John Vanburgh . . . I thought this play would have been more diverting than it proved". Wed. 28th. "False Friend,

Arthur and Emmeline. I shall play this comedy no more, Miss Farren does not like her part, and acts it abominably."

Elizabeth's success and her acceptance in High Society engendered some envy but according to all contemporary sources, any satire steered clear of imputations on her virtue. Gilliland draws attention to the attraction of this side of her character for Lord Derby.

> Her private worth as well as *public* merit had long attracted the admiration of Lord Derby. Though neither his Lordship or Miss Farren were scrupulous to conceal their intimacy, they were cautious in the management of it to give the world *no room for censorious remarks:* and it is observable, that in all their interviews Mrs Farren, who always resided with her daughter, was present in every step of their advancement.[32]

Fresh evidence of the permanent gooseberry! In addition to the warm affection of her many friends, Lord Derby's relatives were all fond of Elizabeth not because she would one day become a member of the family but for her own sweet self. As already shown, Lord Derby was not only attracted by her beauty, charm, wit and good company but by her character and fine feelings.[33]

1. Meister, Henri. Letters written during a Residence in England. 1799. Letter XIV, The English Stage, p.194–202.
2. Ibid
3. Forster, Geo. 1754–1794. p.141
4. Boaden, Siddons p.337
5. Wilkinson, Tate. Op.cit. Vol.ii p.267
6. Ibid. Vol.iii p.48
7. Hotham Papers
8. Wilkinson. Op.cit. Vol.iii. p.86
9. Ibid.
10. Stirling A.M.W. The Hothams. 1918. 2 vols. vol.ii p.227
11. Wilkinson. Tate. Memoirs of his Life. 1790.Vol.i p.122
12. Ibid.
13. Boaden, Siddons p.285
14. Ibid. p.289
15. Boaden, James. Memoirs of Elizabeth Inchbald vol.1 p.174.
    in The Kemble era: John Philip Kemble, Sarah Siddons and the London Stage. (Bodley Head.1980), Mrs Kelly gives the same quotation, (Chapter IV, p.40 para.2) but after Miss Farren, in *curved* brackets are the words (the mistress of the Earl of Derby). On my enquiry she wrote, and I quote, "The brackets should have been squared – and were so in the typescript. The transposition was one of the various misprints which occurred at the proof stage and was unfortunately missed . . . I am annoyed all the same". Mrs Kelly continued, ". . . I suspect though that I drew it from some secondary source and should have checked back . . ." After eight years research I have found no such contemporary statement. Squared brackets tell the reader that the words are those of the author and are not in the quotation.
16. Piozzi. Op. cit. Vol.ii p.734

17. Ibid
18. Kemble's Journals. MSS Manuscript Room. B.M.
19. Ibid.
20. Ibid.
21. Ibid.
22. O'Keefe, John. Recollections. 1826. Vol.2
23. Cloncurry, Lord, V.B. Lawless, Second Baron. Personal Reflections of Life & Times of Ld. Cloncurry 1849.
24. Hotham MSS
25. Ibid.
26. Dublin Evening Post. July 21st 1789.
27. Hotham MSS
28. Kemble MSS
29. Ibid.
30. The Prompter. Nov 4th 1789.
31. Boswell, James Private Papers of; from Malahide Castle. 18 vols ed. G.Scott and F. Pottle 1928–34. Vol.18. Journal 1789-94 p.13.
32. Gilliland, Th. op.cit. Vol.ii p.725
33. Ibid. p.726

Chapter Eight

Thomas Lawrence, the young, up-and-coming painter had recently arrived in London and taken up his abode in Leicester Square to be near the illustrious Sir Joshua Reynolds whose studio was nearby. Reynolds was President of the newly-founded Royal Academy and would soon be appointed as Principal portrait painter to King George III.

Lawrence had been a child prodigy and at a very early age, had been noticed by Mr Prince Hoare on account of his extraordinary aptitude "in drawing that most delicate feature of a likeness, the eye". Indeed it was said to be his most conspicuous quality all his life. John Henry Fuseli deprecated Lawrence's work as a rule but even he said of Lawrence, "he paints eyes better than Titian".

When Lawrence was a boy his father, a failed lawyer, was innkeeper at The Bear Inn, Devizes, where many important travellers broke their journeys to and from fashionable Bath. These included Fanny Burney and Mrs Thrale (later Mrs Piozzi), and many people connected with the theatre. As well as his talent for drawing he had an excellent memory and his father, "was always exhibiting him as a spouter and introducing him to players".[1] It follows that many of the earliest likenesses young Lawrence drew were of actors and actresses of which Mrs Siddons, John Henderson and John Edwin were among the first. So much contact with the theatre combined with reciting long passages from Milton and Shakespeare, gave him a taste for the stage and he decided he wanted to be an actor. This did not suit his father's book at all; he saw his son's lucrative talent going by the board, himself being the loser. When young Thomas fixed up an audition for himself, his father arranged that the test should be rigged and the boy rejected. But Lawrence never lost his interest in the theatre and in players.

When he was nine years old, Thomas Lawrence was given his first box of crayons. The Reverend Dr Henry Kent of Potterne, near Devizes was much annoyed to learn that the boy had drawn a caricature of him on his bedroom wall but was so impressed when he saw it, that he gave Thomas a box of crayons. Before that the boy had only used pencil. A little picture which must have been one of Thomas Lawrence's very first in this medium is a good example of his early genius. On the back of it is written:-

> Rueben requesting of Jacob that Benjamin may goe [sic] down into Egypt. It is his own design which he has drawn himself in Crayens [sic].
> by Thos. Lawrence, aged nine years.[2]

Soon after Lawrence arrived in London he was commissioned to paint Queen Charlotte and while he was at Windsor, he also did a delightful drawing of Mrs Papendiek with her son, Frederick. This was in the autumn of 1789 and early the next year, he began on the famous full length portrait of Elizabeth. This story of the first sitting has come down through the years. It is said that when Elizabeth arrived at Lawrence's studio in Jermyn Street, she pulled off her right glove and put her hand up to her throat to unclasp her cloak. Lawrence is said to have called to her, 'stay as you are' and to have made the preliminary sketch there and then. Looking at the portrait this story could very well be true.[3]

Mrs Papendiek throws some sidelights on circumstances surrounding this portrait.

> While in town I called on Sunday after service with my brother on the Zoffanys who had established themselves in Fitzroy Square, Zoffany having resumed his portrait painting. The painting-room did not exhibit a welcome for not a portrait there except one of his old and sincere friend, Miss Farren – a small whole length, in a green satin dress

and black Spanish hat, (then the costume for dinner-parties). Zoffany was particularly great in drapery, both as regards the folds and taste in copying the elegancies of dress, and this portrait being faultless in these points, and also a keen likeness, was a perfect gem.[4]

On seeing this portrait of Elizabeth, Mrs Papendiek told Zoffany, who had just returned after five years in India, of the portrait young Lawrence was painting of her and that he intended to exhibit it at the Royal Academy. Zoffany replied, 'I shall go and look at it, and if I think by exhibiting it, he will gain credit to himself, I will keep mine back, for a young man must be encouraged'.[5]

Mrs Papendiek then called on Lawrence and his parents and saw the now famous painting. 'Such a likeness, such an exquisite portrait riveted [sic] me to the spot. I said: Zoffany yields the palm to you, and does not mean to exhibit his gem.' Lawrence answered that Zoffany was kind and he felt obliged to him. Then he told Mrs Papendiek that he was in a dilemma and explained, 'Two gentlemen had called to see his pictures and were so struck with the portrait of Miss Farren when only the head was done, that they offered him 100 gns for it, with permission to exhibit it. He answered that Lord Derby having seen it, had at once said he would purchase it for sixty guineas, the price Lawrence had put on it. Lord Derby called often being interested in the progress of the picture, and Lawrence told him of the offer made by the two gentlemen. Lord Derby could only say that he was prepared to keep his Agreement – Mr Lawrence could do as he thought proper.'[6]

According to Mrs Papendiek, Lawrence's father was all in favour of accepting the higher offer, his mother of keeping his word to Lord Derby.

Lawrence was only just twenty-one when his portraits of Queen Charlotte and of Elizabeth were exhibited at the Royal Academy Exhibition in May 1790.

Quickly the portrait of Elizabeth became "Picture of the Year" and at the Private View, Sir Joshua Reynolds, P.R.A., made the generous remark, 'In you Sir, the world will expect to see accomplished what I have failed to achieve'. In the portrait, Elizabeth, tall and graceful with a most engaging expression looks so real and so gay, almost as if she would walk out of the summer landscape in which she is shown.

Comments on the portrait were mainly enthusiastic. The Publick [sic] Advertiser wrote, "such a portrait as that of Miss Farren might excite envy in the mind of the first artist that ever existed. We have seen a variety of portraits of Miss Farren but never before saw her mind and character upon canvas. It is completely Miss Farren, arch, careless, spirited and engaging."[7] The St James' Chronicle was not quite so keen and hinted at the spectre of Elizabeth's leaning towards being affected. "A most spirited resemblance . . . The figure is easy and natural, the affectation of the original is well disguised. The sattin [sic] cloak and fur are admirably painted . . ."[8]

The English Chronicle pronounced it to be a far superior painting to Reynold's Mrs Billington (as St Cecilia), "in spirit, colouring and expression".[9]

Some critics carped at the fact that Elizabeth, though shown in a summer landscape was wearing warm clothes and carried a muff. This upset Lawrence who complained to Edmund Burke, who replied, 'Never mind what the little critics say, for painters' proprieties are always best'. Lawrence was little comforted, especially when the following appeared.

On a Celebrated Picture
of
Miss FARREN

Incas'd in fur; as shrinking from the blast;
Midst scenes that glow with all that summer yields.
Where not a cloud the sky has overcast,
Where blooms the garden, smiles the distant fields
We know thee Farren, by thy lovely face:

But sure the artist ought to shew [sic] some cause
Why thus he sins against all truth and grace
Why thus he turns his back on Nature's laws.

Why thus, pale, shiv'ring on a summer's day,
He paints Thalia's child, all sportive fair and gay.[10]

In spite of public praise, circumstances surrounding the portrait and aspects of the picture itself, did not please Elizabeth. For a start, it was labelled "Portrait of an Actress" which, without a qualifying adjective was tantamount to an insult: an actress was no better than she should be – or such was the implication. It was polite and customary to put "celebrated" or some such complimentary word. Lawrence was accused of an unpardonable *faux pas* but it was not his fault; he had labelled it "Portrait of a Lady", and wrote to Elizabeth explaining that it was the officials of the Royal Academy who had altered "lady" to "actress". In a reprint of the catalogue the word "celebrated" preceded "actress" but that was the only alteration; Lawrence felt the officials had played a spiteful trick on him.

Lord Derby had not commissioned the portrait but had made it clear he would purchase it for sixty guineas. This "misunderstanding" about the price occasioned a letter to Lawrence from Elizabeth.

Sir,

I must own that I was never more astonished in my life than on reading your letter this morning – you must have forgot that last time I had the honour of sitting to you, you told me the price of My Portrait would be sixty guineas, and I then informed you that Lord Derby meant to be the purchaser. It is I trust needless to say more on the subject; you are now (if you can think so after the above) at liberty to put what price you think fit upon the Picture; but you will not think of selling it without my Consent.

I have the honour to remain your humble servt. Eliza Farren.[11]

Lord Derby was two years in private treaty for the portrait and at the end of the day was obliged to pay the extra forty guineas, making the price one hundred guineas. Even then it was not the end of Lawrence's troubles over it. Once the portrait was delivered to Derby House, Elizabeth wrote to him again.

> *Mr Lawrence, you will think me the most troublesome of all human beings, but indeed it is not my fault; they teaze me to Death about this Picture, and insist upon my writing to you.*
>
> *One says it is so thin in the figure that you might blow it away – another that it looks broke off in the middle; in short you must make it a little fatter at all events, and diminish the bend you are so attached to Even if it makes the Picture look ill, for the owner of it is quite distressed about it at present. I am shocked to teaze you, and dare say you wish the portrait in the fire – but as it is impossible to appease the Cries of my friends, I must beg you to Excuse.*[12]

Lawrence made no alterations to the portrait and succeeded in placating Elizabeth by exerting his well-known charm in a letter. His beautiful portrait has been copied in oils, watercolours, pencil and extensive engravings and in the nineteenth century, it was woven in black and white silk to make a small picture about a foot wide.

During this century, very attractive calendars of it were made and although the colours are not exact, they are well worth framing. Up until the early 1920s these and numerous postcards could be freely bought.

All the contemporary reproductions took Elizabeth's beauty and prowess as an actress into countless drawing-rooms and parlours throughout the land so that through them her appearance must have been made more familiar than any other actress and probably, any other woman of her time. The portrait was said to be the turning-point of Lawrence's career.

Lawrence painted at least one other portrait of Elizabeth, a half-length which was commissioned by her mother. In this she was in white silk trimmed with fur. Again she had a muff; the wits said this was symbolic "of a certain noble dangler" so as with his full length, Lawrence must have painted it before Elizabeth's marriage. Her mother kept it but by 1863 it was in Sir Francis Grant's collection. In that year it was sold for only seventy-nine guineas. Twenty-five years later, at the Reginald Cholmondeley sale, it fetched two thousand two hundred and fifty guineas; its present whereabouts are unknown.

It has already been said that Lawrence never lost interest in acting. This is what he says in a letter to his married sister, written on January 28th 1803.

> *My dearest sister,*
> *. . . You have seen in the papers an account of a theatrical fête at the Marquis of Abercorn's.*
> *The Prince, the Duke of Devonshire, Lord and Lady Melbourne, Lord and Lady Essex, with a long etcetera amongst the rest, Sheridan was present . . .*
> *At first, I will own to you, Sheridan's face and the grave Duke of Devonshire, and two or three staunch critics made me feel unpleasantly; for I opened the piece. However this soon wore off.*
> *Lord Abercorn is an old Jermyn Street friend a staunch and honourable one, and particularly kind to me . . .*
> *I am not going to be a performer in other families. I stick to Lord Abercorn's; and for the rest I pursue my profession as quietly and more steadily than ever.*
> *Adieu, dear dear Anne*
>
> > *Ever your attached brother*
> > *Thomas Lawrence.*[13]

Anne Bloxam provided Lawrence with four nieces and six nephews who adored "Uncle Lawrence" as they called him. Always generous to a fault – though ever short of money – he was a by-word for kindness and went to the length of paying for the Oxford education of four of his six nephews: Anne Bloxam called him your "Angel Uncle".

After Sir Thomas Lawrence's death in January 1830 there was a quasi-public funeral at St Paul's Cathedral on the 21st. Etiquette required a chief mourner and a contretemps arose as to whether it should be his brother-in-law, the Reverend Dr R.R. Bloxam or his nephew Richard Rowland Henry Kent Bloxam (named after "Henry Kent", Lawrence's very first patron). In the event, the latter as the eldest "relative in blood", was chosen but not before the Heralds at the College of Arms had pronounced the correct procedure. Their decision was taken from the precedent of the funeral of Sir Willoughby Dixie, marshalled by Sir William Dugdale, Garter King at Arms, in 1670. The question had not arisen for 160 years. The scene of the six Bloxam brothers following their uncle's coffin was sketched in water-colour by the celebrated artist, J.M.W. Turner R.A.[14]

Chapter Eight – Footnotes

1. Patmore, P.G. The Cabinet of Gems. 1837 p.6
2. Written by Sir Thomas Lawrence's nephew, Matthew Bloxam F.S.A., on the back of the picture
3. Lawrence Dr W.J. op.cit. p.98
4. Manners and Williamson. 'Zoffany' 1920
5. Ibid.
6. Papendick Court & Private Life in the time of Queen Charlotte ed. Mrs V. Delves Broughton 1887, vol II p.99.
7. Public Advertiser 30th April 1790
8. St. James' Chronicle 4th May 179
9. English Chronicle 29th April – 1st May 1790
10. Bellamy, Thomas. Miscellanies in Prose & Verse 1795. Vol.ii
11. The Royal Academy of Arts. Library, London. LAW/1/28
12. Layard, Soames. Sir Thomas Lawrence's Letter Bag 1906 p.15
13. Williams D.E., Life & Correspondence of Sir Th. Lawrence P.R.A 1831 p.229. Sir Th. Lawrence to his sister, Mrs Bloxam, wife of The Reverend Dr R. R. Bloxam. Assistant Master, Rugby School.
14. Bloxam Papers (from newspaper cutting of 1877). p.114

Chapter Nine

At last Elizabeth dates a letter to Sir Charles Hotham.

Tuesday, June 9th 1790

I will not attempt to express my good friend, the pleasure I felt on reading your letter this morning; to hear that you are well and as happy as you deserve to be will always give me great delight. Plutarch ascribes to Heraclitus, a saying with which I am mightily taken viz. 'that all men whilst they are awake are in one common world; but that each of them, when he is asleep is in a world of his own.' Now I do perfectly agree with Mr Heraclitus & by this very circumstance I have often seen you all since you left Town, that is in my own little world, and as I can't see you whilst I am awake, I feel very happy to dream of you a little.

And now to answer your enquiries after your Loves. With great and true regret I must inform you that (in my opinion) Love the first [1] (The Hon. Mrs Damer) is not one whit better than when you last saw her and it is with unspeakable sorrow that I see her strength daily growing less and less; but she walks about and does not complain with a Pulse at Ninety! What can one say? you know how difficult it is to hint, & how very unlikely that my hint should be attended to when given. I have great hope from the effects of Country air. She goes to Park Place [2] in about ten or twelve days – I told her your anxieties about her and she sends her best Love, Lady Ailesbury too desires to be kindly remembered to all.

For Love the Second[3] (Mrs Siddons) I can't say much – She is not well, but not so Ill as she has been, she has been at Streatham with the Piozzis ever since Saturday, and I think looks well.

Now for poor Love the third,[4] [Elizabeth herself] she has been Dying, Dear Sir Charles, and is now writing to you with a Blister half a yard long upon her back; "think of me Master Brook! The Deuce take it – here are some fussy People coming to hinder me'.

Wednesday morning.

No: I could never sit down to write again all Day – but here I am once more to go on with my misfortunes, tho' I shall never get so good a Pen as I had yesterday. Even the Ink has changed its Colour on purpose to vex me, it can't be help'd 'on fait se qu'on peut, non pas ce qu'on veut.' Well then, I have been very Ill, but am now getting better, and set off for Scotland next Saturday sen'night! I see you now making de grands yeux, but I am not going to Gretna Green, so you may be quite easy on that Head. Of Kemble I know Nothing, but am very angry with him, as he has not once enquired after me thro' my severe illness. You know we must quarrel about something.

From Her Grace Mary (the Duchess of Richmond) I have a message to you. She says that, from all she can learn, the opera will be at the Old Shop . . .

Is not Lady Dorothy transported that Lord Edward Fitzgerald is returned to Health after all his perils? upon my word, it seem'd quite to turn the Duchess of Leinster's Brain.

People now begin to think we shall have a War – but nothing is known as yet, it is very strongly believd [sic] that Parliament will be dissolved about the 12th of this Month; they have been Playing the Deuce again at Paris; but notwithstanding their intestine broils have fitted out a very considerable Fleet, where it will be destined remains to be decided.

Adieu, Dear Sir Charles, give my love to the dear Ladies, & accept all sorts of kind messages that I am charged with for them & you by all those you Love and Esteem here.

Most truly your affect^{te} friend

Eliza Farren.[5]

This is Elizabeth's first mention of politics, a subject in which she took an increasing interest. The letter shows what friendly terms she was on with the Duchess of Richmond and the next letter to Sir Charles, shows the intimacy she enjoyed with the Hothams.

1790

My Dear Sir Charles,

With your permission and Lady Dorothy's we are coming to Eat you out of House & Home for a few Days; I shall almost be with you before you get this Note, till when I

Remain Dear Sir Charles

Your Most Obliged

Eliza Farren.[6]

Elizabeth had been invited to appear at the Theatre Royal, Edinburgh from June 26th to July 28th, her first visit to Scotland. Plainly she and her mother desired to break their journey at Dalton in Yorkshire with Sir Charles and Lady Dorothy Hotham.

The Scots enjoyed her – and Thomas King who was with her – and comments were all particularly complimentary. After *The School for Scandal* on July 14th the Caledonian Mercury reported.

> Yesterday evening the *School for Scandal* was performed to a crowded audience. The loud and repeated marks of applause given to Mr King and Miss Farren, in the parts of

Sir Peter and Lady Teazle, were the best testimonies of their distinguished excellence in those characters.[7]

Elizabeth's friends continued to be exercised in their minds over her health and on October 16th 1790, Mrs Damer wrote to Sir Charles Hotham, "Miss Farren you have heard from, she , you know, is of the too delicate sort ever long to-gether to enjoy perfect health in the corporal and mental foggs [sic] and boggs [sic] of this sad world".[8] It is true she cannot have been at the top of her form that October for she only acted in five performances between October 11th and 20th. However, In November she was back on form with thirteen performances, beginning on November 1st and ending on the 29th.

In May 1791 there was a flurry of excitement amongst Elizabeth's friends at a report Kemble sent to Sir Charles Hotham – that Lady Derby was dying; Elizabeth, outwardly at any rate, remained calm and unconcerned and ignored the subject when writing to Sir Charles the following month.

June 1791

You are a most Faithless Recreant Knight & do not deserve that I should ever condescend to take any Notice of you; but I am, with a Magnanimity that will astonish you; bribing the Bell-Man to wait till I inform you that the King & Queen of France with the Dauphin have Effected an Escape! They may now cry "Vive la Nation", as loud as they please, for le Roi is out of hearing; all London is full of this News, it arrived late last Night at the Secretary of State's office; and a Hundred Persons have by this time Exactly settled where they are, & what will happen in consequence of their flight, but I am neither wise enough to know one or guess the other, and as my friend the Bell-Man is impatient I hasten to assure you

I am Your very sincerely Angry

Eliza Farren.[8]

128

Alas! History relates that the King and Queen of France were captured at Varennes and brought back to Paris.

Elizabeth is chiding Sir Charles for not coming to London. In fact, although he lived for another three years, his health was poor and he remained in Yorkshire for the rest of his life.

Not one word about the supposed fatal illness of Lady Derby but her apparent indifference was not shared by her friends. Mrs Piozzi impatiently expostulated, 'Will Miss Farren's coronet never be put on?' In the event, Lady Derby lived on for six years.

"They have pulled down Old Drury and are making residence at the fine new Opera House in the Hay Market . . ."[9] So wrote Mrs Piozzi on September 13th, 1791. Sheridan had ordered Henry Holland to demolish the theatre and submit plans for a new and larger Drury Lane. Mrs Piozzi was altogether worried for on the same day she wrote, ". . . If poor Mrs Siddons is sick and Miss Farren – called 'to the Upper House' there will be neither Tragedy nor Comedy".[10] Elizabeth did act Lady Teazle on September 17th and 24th but she did not appear again until October 20th – over three weeks, so illness must have been the cause.

The Drury Lane players did not remain at the Opera House but removed to the Haymarket Theatre where they were directed by George Colman the Younger, his father having died. There on April 3rd 1793, Elizabeth acted in a new comedy, *False Colours*. The Times carried the following on April 6th.

> Mrs Goodall's pad in the new Comedy at the Haymarket is a natural one. It is the effect of nature – not of art. Miss Farren's is the whim of fashion – the new-fangled excrescence which denoted "they wish it so". [11]

Such was the impact of the new fashion – the bustle. Any padding seems to have been frowned on as The Times wrote four days before. [Elizabeth had evidently attended the Trial of Warren Hastings regularly; it was in its fifth year.]

Miss Farren again attended the trial in the Hall, padded above stairs. Miss Markham another actress below. This scandalous fashion will soon be thrust out of repute and indecent.[12]

Elizabeth was always in the height of fashion. George Engleheart painted a charming miniature of her in 1791 in which she is wearing a very fetching saxe blue hat with, "her powdered hair dressed à la conseilleur".[13]

After a particularly strenuous season Elizabeth finished off as Lady Teazle on June 4th 1793; the new theatre was not ready so the performance was at the Haymarket. For nearly a year, Elizabeth did not act again.

It appears that her life of hard work – and she was a perfectionist – had begun to tell on her health and looks. On 16th August Mrs Piozzi wrote to Mrs Pennington (who was not well either) and advised, ". . . the situation of your affairs requires chearful [sic] carriage and gay manners; assume them and they will cling to you. Miss Farren tries that trick and it succeeds too, notwithstanding her *real* health and looks are much impaired, but I hope bathing in the sea may in some measure restore them".[14]

Ever since George III had paid a visit to Weymouth to bathe in the sea, it had become de rigueur and the cure for many ills supposedly. For unknown reasons it was thought best to bathe in the winter and in the early morning! This often in a northern resort such as Scarborough. Wherever she went, sea-bathing failed to cure Elizabeth for, six weeks later, Mrs Piozzi wrote, "Miss Farren alters terribly".[15] Later in the same letter she writes, "Mrs Siddons, after all her lamentions about ill-health looks incomparably handsome I am told"[16] Another difference in character between these two great actresses comes to light – it seems Mrs Siddons was not one to put a good face on troubles.

Mrs Piozzi refers to Elizabeth's health for the last time on January 14th 1794, "Miss Farren was here last week, sadly altered".[17] It is tantalising that there is no way of finding out what was the matter with her; there is no record of her acting – or her whereabouts – between June 4th 1793 and April 1794. Others of the Drury Lane Theatre company either travelled or temporarily retired pending the opening of the new theatre.

Because the date of the opening of the new Drury Lane fell in Lent, there was a concert of Handel's music instead of a play. The seating had been increased from 2,000 to 3,611 and it was considered to be the finest theatre in Europe. It was so enormous that Mrs Siddons called it, "Holland's Wilderness". The nick-name stuck but she evidently liked it for she wrote to Lady Harcourt, "Our new theatre is the most beautiful that imagination could paint. We open with *Macbeth* on Easter Monday".[18] This was April 21st 1794 and although Lady Macbeth was one of Mrs Siddons' exclusive parts, she told Lady Harcourt, "You cannot conceive what I feel at the prospect of playing there. I dare say I shall be so nervous as scarcely to be able to make myself heard in the first scene".[19]

On Monday April 21st, new Drury Lane was packed to overflowing. Kemble played *Macbeth* but although Elizabeth was better, she was not up to a part and George Colman the Younger, "got up a pantomime epilogue most gaily for Miss Farren, who, when delivering it assumed the character of a housekeeper to some titled virtuoso".[20]

> .... who
> Permits the envious crowd his house to view
> When pictures, busts, and bronzes to display
> He treats the public with a public day;
> That all the world may in their minds retain them
> He bids his dawdling housekeeper explain them.

131

Our pile is rock, more durable than brass,
Our decoration gossamer and gas;
Weight, yet airy in effect; our plan
Solid – tho' light, – images yet unborn,
Our castle's strength shall laugh a siege to scorn!
The very ravages of fire we scout,
For we have wherewithal to put it out.
In ample reservoirs our firm reliance
Whose streams set conflagration at defiance.
Panic alone avoid, – let none begin it
Should the flames spread, sit still there's nothing in
it:-
We'll undertake to drown you all in half a minute!

At this point Elizabeth waved a wand and a huge iron safety curtain, covering the stage opening was lowered, leaving her between it
and the footlights while she declaimed –

The hottest fire shan't a singe a single feather.
No. I assure our generous benefactors,
We'll only burn the scenery and the actors.[21]

After these reassuring lines, Elizabeth was loudly cheered – not
least perhaps because it was her first appearance before the public
since June 4th the previous year. The safety curtain was now raised
showing a lake of real water on the stage with a man rowing a boat
across it while the band struck up Charles Dibdin's rousing tune, The
Jolly Young Waterman.

For all these protective measures Drury Lane was gutted fifteen
years later. Sheridan was a Member of Parliament then and was in
the Commons while the fire raged, having refused an adjournment of
the debate. Later, watching the fire, bottle in hand, he made the
remark, "Cannot a man take a glass of wine at his own fireside?"

Mrs Piozzi was lucky to be alive to attend the opening of Holland's
Wilderness as she wrote to Mrs Pennington.

. . . Meanwhile I had like to have been made a speedy end of, Thursday last week, by a bone in my throat, which called Surgeons and Doctors around me, and all in vain, for three long hours. Poor Miss Farren, who was with me, seemed half killed by the fright, but all is safe and well again.

What an alarming experience for the compassionate Elizabeth.[22]

During the remainder of the Drury Lane season, Elizabeth often repeated the Epilogue she had spoken at the opening of the new theatre – sometimes, "By particular Desire . . ." as on May 9th, the first night of Richard Cumberland's *The Jew*. This was an attempt by him to put the Jews in a better light but it was only moderately successful. Elizabeth played the heroine, Louisa Radcliffe. She must have recovered her health for she worked extremely hard up till her final performance of the season on June 21st. Shortly afterwards she and her mother would be setting off on another journey to Ireland, not only to Dublin but to Cork and Limerick as well. Richard Daly, who invited her, was the manager of Crow Street Theatre in Dublin, the Theatre Royal in Cork and the Theatre Royal in Limerick.

When Elizabeth went to Dublin in 1794, her young second cousin, Charles Farran Junior, was not there. He was in India, an ensign in the 27th battalion Native Infantry, fighting in the Mysore Wars against Tippoo Sahib. The journey had taken nearly two years and there had been what he called an "unpardonable" silence before he wrote a long letter to his father from "Camp near Osoor" on 14 August, 1791. He explains that "being in the field in Tippoo's Country, prevents any correspondence except two or three lines roll'd in a Quill". This letter is eight foolscap pages long, full of interesting details of battles, the country and important military figures, including the poisoning of General Mathews, "with a number of other English Officers".

Promotion at that time depended largely on influence and Elizabeth and Lord Derby had written to many important friends on

Charles' behalf. He had of course, written to thank her but in a letter to her from Cassimcottah of September 17th he says:-

> My Dear Cousin,
> I received a letter about one Month since from my Father
> in which he mentions his Surprize [sic] that I had not
> written to you which vexed me exceedingly – to find the
> Letters I had written to you had Miscarried as I must
> have been not only a Most Ungratefull [sic] (which I hope
> will never be the Case) Fellow, but also very Negligent of
> my own future Welfare & advancement in this Country
> which depends much on your friendly assistance which I
> have already experienced in a very great Degree &
> which I shall always remember with Gratitude –

After discussing some of the help he has received from Elizabeth's contacts, Charles goes on:-

> My principle [sic] wish to succeed in this Country is to be
> of service hereafter to my Family (as I believe I shall be
> the Old Batchelor [sic] of it) as the Ladies that come out
> to this Country are in General of a Dubious Character and
> I do not see any Prospect of Going Home for a Number of
> Years . . .

In fact, he married twice and had a large family!

Describing Cassimcottah Charles says:-

> This Cantonment is a most beautiful Place, about twelve
> Miles from the Sea – We have Plenty of Wild fowl from
> the Neighbouring Lakes (which are very extensive) &
> Fish from the Sea . . . we pass our time very pleasantly
> and I should say contentedly if the Idea of the
> Separation from our Relations did not frequently Occur . . .
> The usual mode of Killing Time particularly in the Hot
> Season is Lounging from Breakfast until Dinner on a Couch

134

which Debilitates the Constitution so much that I never Practice [sic] it. I have been endeavouring to obtain a Muster Mastership . . .

Towards the end of the letter Charles writes,

I would be highly gratified if opportunity should enable me to send you a few pieces of Muslin but as yet I am so far out of the Way that I have not been able to get any safe Person to take charge of them and I cannot send them otherwise as they are contraband.

I shall esteem it a Favor [sic] if you will present my Grateful acknowledgements to Lord Derby whom I hope is in as Good Health as I wish him . . . The Heat of the Weather and the Musquitoes [sic] together have made me make a number of mistakes which I hope you will excuse – Pray make my respectful Compliments to your Good Mother and Believe me with the Sincerest esteem and regard –

Your Affectionate Cousin
Cha^{rs} Farran.[23]

The muslin - some gold, some silver – is mentioned in every letter home; it went from battle to siege to battle in Charles' baggage until he found "a safe Person" but it reached Elizabeth in the end. It was some of his plunder from the siege of Bangalore which included "5 shawls for my Mother".

Charles was a very affectionate man and adored his father and mother. Frequently he interrupts his letters with, "Please give my Love and Duty to my Dear Mother," and through his loving messages to his many brothers and sisters as well as brothers-in-law and sisters-in-law, all their nick-names are known.

He was "in the field" most of the time with Lord Cornwallis in his campaign against Tippoo, the Tiger of Mysore. He told his father, "and have thank God escaped unhurt except a slight scratch on my

Leg with a Musket Ball". He became a Major-General and when he retired, settled in Parambore, Madras, where he died on June 29th 1842, having been in India for 52 years. "Farran's Road", Pursewaukum, is named after him. In the map of 1822 his house is marked, "Colonel Farr*en*" and in that of 1837, "Major-General Farr*on*"; two erroneous spellings of his signature, "Farran".[24]

Two mutual cousins in the East India Company Army are mentioned in all Charles Farran's letters, William and James Achilles Kirkpatrick, sons of Captain James Kirkpatrick of the Madras Cavalry. William was an expert in Oriental languages, several times interpreter to high-ranking officers in Persian, including Lord Cornwallis who was both commander-in-chief and Governor-General of India. William and his staff were the first Englishmen to go to Nepal; he was chosen to go to the Court there to negotiate between the Nepalese and Chinese in 1793. Later he became Resident at Hyderabad and afterwards, Confidential Secretary to Lord Mornington, (brother of the Duke of Wellington) when he was Governor-General of India, as Baron Wellesley. Wellesley had such a high opinion of William Kirkpatrick that he said he was "unequalled by any man he had ever met in India".

James Achilles Kirkpatrick was a most romantic and dashing figure and a fine soldier. Educated at Eton and in France, he entered the Madras Army at sixteen and he too had the full confidence of Baron Wellesley. In a letter to Elizabeth, Charles Farran wrote, "Lieut. James Kirkpatrick told me he saw you when he was at Home. We are fortunately always near each other and have frequent opportunities of cultivating an intimacy that we are bound by the ties of consanguinity to improve".[25]

He was responsible for many negotiations including bringing 60,000 of the Nizam of Hyderabad's army into the field on the English side against Tippo.

The real fascination of James Achilles Kirkpatrick was his marriage to a high-born and beautiful Indian, Khair-un-Nissa, niece of the Nizam of Hyderabad where James had become the Resident in place of his brother, William. It was said that the ceremony was according to Moslem rites. The English Government and the East India Company were displeased – marriage with Indians was discouraged; it was felt the wives might exert undesirable influence on their husbands. Baron Wellesley enquired into the matter and there were strong rumours that James would be dismissed the service

– but he was too valuable and remained as Resident of Hyderabad.

For a time the tale unfolded in fairytale fashion. James built a beautiful palace-cum-residency with a great hall, sixty feet long, thirty-four wide and half the height of the nave of Canterbury Cathedral. Furnishings included fine gilt mirrors and chandeliers bought from the Prince Regent. The upper floor was reached by a marble staircase in an apse at the far end of the hall which divided, each side curving upwards to the balcony-passages above. The zenana, where the Princess lived in seclusion, had beautiful paintings on the walls and was cooled with playing fountains.

An extensive park with roaming deer, an Abyssinian goat and an elk, surrounded the palace. There was a walled fruit garden and a separate flower garden filled with lovely and unusual blooms, not endemic to India.

The eccentric James was popular with Indians and English alike; he dressed in Oriental clothes, sported "moustachies" and dyed his fingers with henna. The Nizam gave him the vernacular name, "Hashmut Jung" – the magnificent in battle – and George Chinnery painted him in full-dress uniform of pale blue with silver-braid strapping. A boy and a girl were born, a well sunk to mark the birth of each. When they were still very small, the fairytale ended – their father decided they must go to his father and brother William, at Bromley in Kent, and be educated in England. And so it was. Their beautiful mother was distraught and she made two stipulations. First their portrait was to be painted by George Chinnery who had already painted their father and second, ten thousand pounds settled on each child. These wishes carried out they sailed for England in the care of a trusted Indian servant.

James Achilles Kirkpatrick had asked that the first thing to be done was to give them a Christian baptism with English names. The girl's name in English meant, "Our Little Princess and English Lady"; she was christened Catherine Aurora; the little boy, "The Little Lord of the World", George William. Poor little things; one wonders what ever can their feelings have been, translated from such oriental splendour to Bromley, though no doubt it was country then. Their parents died – perhaps their father had a premonition as he only lived one month after they sailed – they never returned to India but their grandmother, Sharif-un-Nissa, sent letters to them in Persian, each sprinkled with gold dust and enclosed in a "kharita" – a little gold brocade bag – before sending it to England.

Catherine Aurora is the "Kitty Kirkpatrick" of Thomas Carlyle's *Reminiscences*, (Published 1881 after Carlyle's death) and comes in many of his writings under different names and in different guises. He met her on the first night of his arrival in London from Scotland, "a strangely-complexioned young lady, with soft brown eyes and floods of bronze-red hair, really pretty-looking, smiling and amiable".[26] He was in love with her. At another time he wrote that although, "she was sole mistress of 50,000 1.{pounds} she is meek and unassuming as a little child".[27] She plainly fascinated Carlyle.

James Achilles Kirkpatrick died on a journey to Bengal at the early age of 41, and is buried in the South Parks Cemetery, Calcutta, with a fine monument, inscribed as follows:-

> To the memory of Lt. Col. James Achilles Kirkpatrick of the Honourable East India Co's military establishment of Fort St George who after filling the distinguished station of Resident at Hyderabad upwards of nine years and successfully conducting during that period various important negotiations, died at Calcutta 15th October 1805, aged 41.
>
> This monument is erected by his afflicted father and brother.[28]

Seldom can an epitaph have concealed more effectively the real man.

1. Mrs Damer
2. Park Place, Lady Ailesbury's House at Henley-on-Thames
3. Mrs Siddons
4. Elizabeth herself
5. Hotham MSS
6. Ibid
7. Caledonian Mercury July 15th 1790
8. Hotham MSS
9. Piozzi. op.cit. p.821
10. Ibid.
11. The Times, April 6th 1793
12. The Times, April 12th 1793
13. Sotheby's Catalogue, July 20th 1981 (this minature was sold that day for £1,400)
14. Piozzi. The Intimate Letters of Hester Piozzi & Penelope Pennington 1788-1821 Ed. Oswald Knapp 1913 p.97
15. Ibid. p.98
16. Ibid. p.98
17. Ibid. p.98
18. Campbell T. Life of Mrs Siddons 1834. Letter to Lady Harcourt 11th April 1794 p.183
19. Ibid. p.183
20. Adolphus op.cit. Vol.i p.335
21. Ibid. p.336
22. Piozzi op.cit (Pennington Letters) p.110
23. All references in a letter to Eliz. Farren from her second cousin, Charles Farran jnr. of 17th September 1793. (Farran papers & letters.)
24. Love, H. Davidson. Vestiges of Old Madras
25. See note 23
26. Froude J.A. Thomas Carlyle: The First Forty Years 1882. p.241

27. Ibid.
28. Cotton, Julian James. Inscriptions on Tombs or Monuments in Madras possessing Historical or Architectural Interest 1905. p.2308

Chapter Ten

Elizabeth's last performance in the Drury Lane season was as Louisa Radcliffe in *The Jew* on June 21st. She cannot have had much rest as the actor, Charles Mathews wrote in Dublin on June 27th, "Miss Farren is expected every day. She will draw very crowded houses as the boxes for her nights are extremely well taken."[1] Nothing of where she and her mother stayed is known. Certainly they would have been entertained by Charles Farran senior, her father's cousin, who had now held the important post of Deputy Clerk of the Pleas in the Court of the Exchequer in Dublin for twelve years. He had sat recently for his portrait to the eminent American portratist Gilbert Stuart who had painted many of consequence during his time in Ireland. He painted a companion portrait of Charles' second wife, Sarah née Orson, of Londonderry. Stuart also painted Elizabeth and all three portraits are now in the United States.

Elizabeth and her mother would have had hospitality too from Charles and Sarah's eldest son, Joseph and his wife, known as "the beautiful Miss Lambert of the County Wicklow branch." Like his father, Joseph was a lawyer and, also like his father, his town house was in York Street.[2]

Crow Street Theatre in Dublin, where Elizabeth was to appear, was nearly as large as New Drury Lane. The Manager was Richard Daly, whose wife, a Miss Barsanti – a good actress – had won a lottery and generously gave Daly the money to enlarge and improve the theatre. When it was ready, he copied Thomas Sheridan of the now defunct Smock Alley Theatre, inviting meritorious players over from England including not only Elizabeth but Kemble and Mrs Siddons. The latter had a dreadful journey arriving in the middle of the night feeling very sick and tired to find that none of the Dublin hotels would admit women!

English players enjoyed visiting Ireland. Macready had written of the "glowing sympathy" of Irish audiences and before him, Samuel Foote, who was popular both on the Irish and the English stage, said his visits to Ireland were "pure profit, pleasure and reputation." From Elizabeth's letter in 1789, it was learned what a wonderful reception she had "which I could never forget if I lived for a thousand years!"

Irish theatre managers were annoyed that audiences insisted on having English players with the "London stamp" because it greatly increased their expenses. Sometimes English players had to be bribed to leave London. Occasionally, too, difficulties over the choice of plays in London were not always well received in Dublin and vice versa. The veteran actor and playwright Charles Macklin said, "I believe the audiences are right, there is a geography in humour as well as in morals which I had not previously considered."[3] This after his *The Trueborn Irishman* flopped in London having been a great success in Dublin.

On July 2, Elizabeth made her first appearance at Crow Street as Lady Bell in Murphy's *Know Your Own Mind* and Mathews predicition was confirmed. "Miss Farren has been all the fashion and nothing else would draw money[3]" Poor young Mathews – he was only seventeen at the time – was cast as Beaufort, "a puling sentimental lover" opposite Elizabeth's "elegant easy figure and accomplished manners" as Maria in *The Citizen*. Got up in a scarlet coat for a man a head shorter, his appearance drew an "American war-whoop" from the audience. After the performance Elizabeth kindly expressed her concern and apologized to him for having been an unwilling accessory to the ridicule his unpractised manner and appearance created.[4] With her soft-heartedness she had made a conquest for life.

Her triumph in Dublin led to the extension of twelve nights engagement to sixteen which cut the number of appearances in Cork and delayed her first appearance there to August 18th. That night she acted Bizarre in *The Inconstant* and opposite her was the wild and attractive Daly himself. They must have made a striking couple. After the Cork visit, Mathews records, "The house has been crowded each night she has played. She was never here before and is very well received and each of her performances brings in about 200/".[5] Boxes cost 4/-, seats in the pit 3/- and the gallery 2/- so it took a good crowd to add up to £200.

In Cork, Daly and Elizabeth had a display by young Mathews of his talent for mimicry and paid him a number of compliments especially for his "Kemble as Octavian."

From Cork the company went to Limerick where the Theatre Royal was very small, only holding 130 people. It had an unuusually small stage and no green-room. Fearing Elizabeth's probable vexation at the inadequate facilities, Daly built a special dressing-room for her which would be the green-room for the future.

The Assizes were on in Limerick when Elizabeth appeared on the first night, September 9th, as Lady Bell in *Know Your Own Mind*. This is Mathews' description.

> She was most rapturously received by a very elegant
> audience, for besides numerous people of fashion residing
> near Limerick, the assizes brought together an immense
> number of people.

He goes on to give the list she played for the rest of her six nights there – a different part each night and an amusing story concerning the last play, Mrs Centlivre's *The Wonder* in which Elizabeth would play Donna Violante. The actor for the hero, Lissardo, had not arrived and the part was assigned to Mathews at a few hours notice.

> I therefore sallied forth to walk and learn on the bank of
> the Shannon in the sultry weather.

He met Seymour, another actor who was similarly engaged in learning his part and then walked on. Soon he was so hot that he thought he would bathe to cool off and not thinking he would be out of his depth in any part of the river, he stripped and walked in. But the water washed over his head and he screamed. It washed over his head a second time and he screamed again but nobody heard him.

> a thousand distressful thoughts. But oh! the ruling passion, strong in death – dare I confess it? – my mind was occasioned for a brief second by conjecturing who could act Lissardo that night if I drowned?[6]

This thought lent strength to Mathews third cry and this time, Seymour heard him. Mathews continues the narration:-

> he was an expert swimmer, and made for the spot where he had last seen me rise, when, in almost despair of rescuing, or even finding me, he felt his legs suddenly seized with violence, and he was dragged by my dying struggles, feeble as they were, to the bottom.

Seymour managed to propel the near-drowned boy to the bank where two soldiers were watching the drama and instructed them to carry the naked Mathews to the nearest public house. Mathews concludes:-

> and I was rescued by the means prescribed by the humane society of Whiskey dealers. (Rubbing vigorously with poteen). "Don't trust the poteen near the mouth of the cratur [sic], or he'll leave you none for the rubbing" said Seymour. Their means were effectual, and I acted Lissardo with the accomplished Farren that night.

That was on Elizabeth's last night in Limerick and in Ireland. She would go home on the following day, Sunday, September 15th. Mathews wrote that he was very sorry to lose her, "for she is one of the most agreeable women I ever saw, and behaves as politely to an underling as to a first rate actor."; he was sorry too that her Limerick benefit was a "thin night". "This was the only thin house she has played to since she has been in Ireland . . . but she cannot complain for she has carried away an immense sum of money. Daly has paid her £50 a night. She played sixteen nights in Dublin, six in Cork, six in Limerick and made two capital benefits."[7]This adds up to £1,400 not counting her benefits – an enormous sum for the eighteenth century.

Comments in Irish papers were enthusiastic. Before Elizabeth played in *Rule a Wife and Have a Wife* as Estifania, The Dublin Evening Post wrote:-

> In compliance with universal desire she comes forward in this favourite character on Monday next "to charm our eyes, our ears, and our understanding." It was universally conceded that as much rank and fashion as had ever honoured the theatre had been the order of the day and that Elizabeth's visit "will ever be remembered by every admirer of the Drama."[8]

While away, Elizabeth kept in touch with Lord Derby and other friends so there was alarm when there was an ominous silence at the end of the Irish visit.

> Miss Farren is missing. She is known to have landed last Sunday – not a word from her since, and makes one – ay, and two – fear that she is ill on the road. Were it her mother, she herself would have written.[9]

The Sunday Walpole referred to was September 22nd and were it not for a paragraph in The Times, one might have thought that the equinoctial gales had caused delay. Not so. Walpole's fears were confirmed; Elizabeth was lying dangerously ill with a high fever at Shrewsbury, attended by three doctors who "despaired of her survival".[10]

Nothing further is known except that she was unable to appear at Drury Lane until November 5th 1794, over six weeks since she arrived back in England.

Ozias Humphrey drew a pastel of Elizabeth which was exhibited at the Royal Academy Summer Exhibition of 1794, but according to Dr W. J. Lawrence, it is not the one "which found its way to Dublin 1889 . . . , the only portrait of the actress in a public collection . . . the sketch with all its merits is not a work of sufficient distinction and completeness to warrant any such supposition. It is none the less desirable, however because it is lacking in that pensive languor so characteristic of Humphrey's women, although the sign-manual of the artist is to be seen in the well-known gazelle-like eye. The face, with its agressive nose, has more of character than of beauty, but it beams with animation and intelligence."[11]This pastel now hangs in Malahide Castle, Co. Dublin – part of the National Gallery of Ireland. In spite of the affirmation by Dr Kenneth Garlick, then Keeper of Western Art at the Ashmolean Museum, Oxford, that it *is* Elizabeth Farren, it carries the caption, "Mrs Siddons."

Elizabeth's first appearance after her illness was as Julia in *The Rivals*, on November 5th, but she was not acting as many performances as usual – only seven in all that November and six in December. By January 1795 she was in full swing again and as much taken up with her social life too. The critics continued to sing her praises. "Miss Farren possesses great merit as an actress and is indisputably the best representative of a Fine Lady now in the London Theatres." Later, William Hazlitt, the greatest dramatic critic of the age would write of "her fine-lady airs and graces, that elegant turn of the head and motion of her fan and tripping of her tongue."[12] She was a long way now, after seventeen years on the London stage from the strictures of the dramatic censor after her debut in 1777.

Lord Derby had been constant for almost as long and as assiduous in his attentions as ever, always solicitous of her well-being. Although good-looking as a younger man, he could not boast anything of good looks now, but he made up for it with great personal magnetism and charm. He needed to, if this contemporary description is anything to go by!

Lord Derby was a singular-looking man for a lover. Although at the time but 45 he looked fifteen years older. He had an excessively large head surmounting his small, spare figure and wore his hair in a long, thin pigtail. This with his attachment to short nankeen gaiters, made him an easily recognised subject in numerous charactures [sic] of the day.[13]

(Nankeen was a cloth of yellow colour, natural to the wool of which it was made).

Horace Walpole's letters give many names included in a long list of mutual friends of Lord Derby's and Elizabeth's. He himself often supped in the same company, theatrical or aristocratic. Curiously, Lord Derby seemed happy to accept invitations from the Kembles and Siddons but it was most noticeable that he never invited them back.

Bond Street had been inexistence for over seventy years – New Bond Street was built just before Grosvenor Square where Lord Derby lived. James Branton wrote this couplet in 1729:

Pease, cabbages and turnips grew where
Now stands New Bond Street and a newer Square.

Bond Street was the most attractive and fashionable shopping street in London – if not in Europe – and Lord Derby and Elizabeth were often seen there à trois, with her mother of course. On one occasion they seem to have shaken her off for a preview of a sale at Christies in King Street, This is the subject of a caricature by James Gillray called: A Peep at Christies . . . or Tally-Ho & his Nimeny-pimeny taking the Morning Lounge.

It is dated 1796, and shows a fashionably dressed, elongated Elizabeth, peering through a pair of elegant red binoculars, held in her green-gloved hand. Tiny Lord Derby in a blue hunting jacket, breeches, boots and spurs is at her side; they both clutch catalogues. (Tally-Ho was in respect of Lord Derby's hunting interests and

Nimeny-pimeny the nickname for Lady Emily Gay-ville, Elizabeth's part in General Burgoyne's play, *The Heiress*).

The two inseparables were not always on the gad as Walpole writes to Mary Berry.

> . . . walked into my room. General Conway. In the evening we went together to Miss Farren's and besides her duenna-mother, found her at Piquet with her unalterable Earl. Apropos, I have observed that when Earls take strong attachments, they are more steady than other men.[14]

Here Walpole was patting himself on the back; he was now Earl of Orford and had long been faithful to Mary Berry.

Whenever Walpole wrote of Elizabeth's mother – "La Signora Madre" as he sometimes calls her, it is clear that wherever the social circle supped she was there, be it with the Duke and Duchess of Richmond or perhaps the Kembles. "Mrs Farren never either in society or in public (except upon the stage – quitted the presence of her matchless daughter."[15] But there is no question of her being a silent chaperone in the background.

Far from having exhausted their stock of praise after so many years of triumphs, Elizabeth had two particularly complimentary comments in 1795.

> . . . her person, excepting being rather too tall, is peculiarly well formed for the sphere of acting in which she moves, and the inexpressible graces that uniformly attends her deportment, give a luxuriant feast to the beholder he never receives from any other performer.
>
> Her countenance is bewitchingly beautiful, with eyes of the most expressive softness, and a voice distinct, clear and harmonious. She is in our opinion the only female on the stage that can give us a proper idea of the real polished woman of fashion, in which she is very little inferior to any other actresses.[16]

These verses appeared at the same time.

With lively air, impressive face,
A form of symmetry and grace;
With all that speaks: (and praise apart)
That speaks a good and gentle heart.
We hail thee Farren; winning maid, –
In Nature's ornaments array'd.
When time mark'd Abington retir'd
You gave what Teazle then requir'd
You fill'd and sweetly look'd the part,
And won Thalia's beating heart,
Till then, fair nymph, the sisters twain
By turns, had held her in their train;
By turns, their higher scenes were grac'd
By turns their Farren they embrac'd.[17]

Despite Elizabeth's firm place in the admiration and affection in the eyes of the public, she lacked the confidence to play the part of Nobody in a comedy of the same name. She refused to act, preferring to pay the necessary fine for withdrawing and saying "that she might continue to be thought Somebody". The play was a failure and hissed throughout; it only survived three performances.

In 1795, Cumberland's new comedy *The Wheel of Fortune* was produced on March 28th, with Elizabeth as the heroine, Emily Tempest. According to Kemble it was received with great applause and, for the very first time since her arrival in London ten years before, Mrs Jordan acted a part in the same play as Elizabeth. Cumberland was very pleased with the play's success and diplomatically used the epithet "exquisite" to describe both actresses.

Great changes took place in the company at Covent Garden in the autumn of 1795 and Elizabeth's sister – Peggy Knight – and her husband, were two of the newcomers, succeeding Edwin and Mrs Wells as Jacob and Bridget in *The Chapter of Accidents*. This drew the comment from Boaden. "Mr Knight . . . was a just, critical actor, and literally analysed a part in the most scientific margins a play-book ever displayed. His wife was the sister of Miss Farren, and had a *strong* resemblance of the beautiful countenance of that delightful actress. She, however remained at an immense distance from her powers in the art."

The next year, 1796, Lord Derby was worried about his daughter, Lady Charlotte Stanley who was bent on marrying her cousin, Edmund Hornby – a young man of whom he very much disapproved. He did his best to persuade them that they "had better see more of the world etc., etc.," but they would not take any notice. Reluctantly Lord Derby gave his consent, generously settling £1,000 a year on Edmund Hornby.

Lady Charlotte was just as devoted to her future step-mother as Lord Stanley and made a great gesture of affection for all the world to see by inviting Elizabeth to be a bridesmaid at her wedding.[18] Accordingly, in the middle of August, Elizabeth set off for Knowsley, chaperoned as usual by her mother and fulfilled her happy duty to her future step-daughter.

> On Monday last, by the Rev. Geoffrey Hornby, in the Domestic Chapel at Knowsley, Edmund Hornby Esq. to Lady Charlotte Stanley, daughter of the Earl of Derby.[19]

Edmund Hornby was a lawyer and the young couple settled into a house in Bedford Row; Lord Derby was to rue the day he had given his consent to the marriage.

Joseph Farington was at Knowsley for the wedding. "Lord Derby's attachment to Miss Farren is extraordinary. He sees her daily and always attends the play when she performs," reads an extract from his diary. He also remarks that her mother is always with her, "so careful is she of appearances."[20]

The finances of Drury Lane in the autumn and winter of 1795 were in an even more parlous state than usual, "the house was overwhelmed with debt, the salaries often unpaid, the distracted state of concern was obvious". A contributory factor was the huge sum paid out to house the company during the rebuilding of the theatre, a total of £11,000, quite apart from the expense of running a London play-house.There was a rumour that Elizabeth was jealous of a new actress, Miss Decamp (later Mrs Charles Kemble), and of a tiff over a "satin-gown" between them. It is more likely that the shortage of money led to an incident in Elizabeth's career which was most unusual to say the least – she failed to turn up in time to dress for the first night of a new comedy, *The Force of Ridicule*, by Holcroft. Boaden paints the scene and illustrates Elizabeth's popularity and the quite extraordinaary patience of an eighteenth century audience.

> The usual time of commencing passed over, and the prologue not appearing to be addressed, the drowsy orchestra having renewed again and again the usual symphonies of Handel, and Shaw having laid down his fiddle in despair – at length Mr Palmer, a countenance of alarm and concern assumed for the nonce, told them that "owing to some unforeseen accident, Miss FARREN had not come to the theatre (the very chronometer of the house!) *but* that a messenger had been dispatched, to know the *reason* of her absence, and the proprietors humbly hoped the audience would indulge them for a few minutes until the messenger returned. About seven o'clock, back came Palmer again, au desespoir, that Miss Farren was 'too ill to leave her room,' but that the audience, who heard nothing for three long hours, but the first women and the fiddlers, might take their money at the doors, or Mrs Siddons as Isabella; and accordingly some did one thing and some the other."[21]

Mrs Siddons was sent for. She was in the audience at Covent Garden at the time – but although she complied with the summons, there had been a mass exodus. When she arrived the theatre was all but empty.

Next day, apparently to save the face of the management, there was a paragraph in the papers, upholding Elizabeth's indisposition, but Boaden gave the truth, "there was but one *chance* of getting *a* considerable sum of arrears in her salary, she seized upon the new comedy as an occasion to give the proprietors notice that "if she did not receive her *money* she would not leave her house". Accordingly, she kept her word better than they did – and *theirs* and the play stood over till 6th December. That time Elizabeth won the day – but not the next time.

This trouble also happened in 1796. A performance of *The Provoked Husband* with Elizabeth in her celebrated rôle of Lady Townley was billed, but although her first appearance in that character had been in August 1778, the theatre was so parsimonious as to decree she should wear the same old dress. She examined it and pronounced herself so dissatisfied with its condition that she took a stand and refused to wear it. Both sides remained immovable and the play was advertised to be withdrawn. Elizabeth was adamant and it was rumoured that she threatened to retire forthwith. On the night when *The Provoked Husband* should have been acted, there was a riot in the theatre with loud calls for Elizabeth, the inference being that she *must* play Lady Townley in rags or not. She was not in the theatre, and an apology was made for her absence, but green-room gossip spread quickly, and everyone was well aware of the ins and outs of the dispute. They refused to be quelled until a promise had been extracted from the management to produce *The Provoked Husband* with Elizabeth in her part on an early, specified night – November 22nd.

When the night arrived, the theatre was filled to suffocation all wishing to see who had won the day but, "Miss Farren not-withstanding her fame, her talents and her prospects, had found the impossibility of contending against the management, which was supported by the public; she not only appeared in the despised satin dress, but was compelled to make an apologetic curtsey to the angry audience before they would allow the play to go on."[22]

Inevitably the situation invited satire, a caricature called "A Peep

Behind the Curtain at the Widow" with two verses, the first spoken by Elizabeth and the second by Lord Derby. (Elizabeth is naked, Lord Derby looking down on her having pulled a curtain aside).

> Here I stand a fresh proof of the Manager's Meanness
> Not a rag to my back like the Medici's Venus
> At their second-hand wardrobe I turn up my Nose
> By the Lord I wont act till they find me new Cloathes [sic]

> O fye [sic] ye Linleys, curse your niggard Hearts
> Why wont you let Miss Farren dress her Parts
> Were I of Drury's property the Sovereign
> I'd give the lovely Maiden choice of Covering.

(The Linleys had a share of Drury Lane with Sheridan).[23]

The year before that ignominious happening, a new young actress, Harriot Mellon, had arrived at Drury Lane. Very soon she idolised Elizabeth, calling her "the great lady" and applying the epithet, "the glass of fashion and the mould of form."[24] Harriot Mellon's biographer wrote that she derived much professional benefit from "her intercourse with the most elegant actress on the stage, whose refined readings of Lady Teazle, and the most elevated class of comedy are to this day quoted as beyond attainment."(This was written more than thirty years after Elizabeth's retirement).

Elizabeth liked Harriot Mellon and one evening the young girl saw another side to her "great lady" in the green-room. She was humming a tune by the fire, tapping the rhythm with her toes when she heard Elizabeth whispering 'You happy girl, I would give worlds to be like you.' Harriot was distressed and disturbed. She, who earned 30/- a week, how could she be envied by her idol? It seemed incredible when Elizabeth earned 18 guineas a week and would one day be a countess. She felt perhaps she was being ridiculed and, vexed, she said, 'there must be a vast deal to be envied by one who commanded what she pleased.' But she had misjudged Elizabeth who pressed her hand and said 'I cannot command as *light heart* as prompted by your little song.'[25]

The Monthly Mirror of November 1796 carried an article on Elizabeth which discussed her attributes and acting in greater depth than had ever been done.

> . . . She is now in her highest excellence of action, happy in all the rarely-found requisites that meet in one person to complete her for the stage . . . of a lively aspect, and a command in her mien, thus like the principal figure in the finest painting, first seizes, and longest delights the eye of the spectators. Her voice is sweet and melodious; her pronunciation voluble, distinct and musical; and her emphasis always placed where the spirit of the sense, in her periods, only demands it . . . The spectator is always as much informed by her *eyes* as her elocution; for the look is the only proof that an actor rightly conceives what he utters, there being scarce an instance, where the *eyes* do their part, that the elocution is known to be faulty. The qualities she has acquired are the genteel and the elegant; the one in her air, the other in her dress, never had her equal on the stage; and the ornaments she herself provides seem in all respects the *paraphernalia* of a woman of quality; and of that sort are the characters she chiefly excels in; but her natural good sense and lively turn of conversation, make her way so easy to ladies of the highest rank, that it is a less wonder if, on the stage, she sometimes is, what may become the finest woman in real life to support . . . The affability of her manners, they will be most inclined to dwell on to whom she is most *known* – if her private character has ever been traduced, it has been by those who know her *not*.[26]

The gossips were bored, tired and disappointed with Elizabeth's exemplary conduct; they had no food for scandal. In general, the public's interest in her private life lay dormant.

Suddenly it was fully awakened – Lord Derby's estranged wife had died on March 14th 1797. The news was not unexpected as she had been in ill-health for six or more years. Extravagant throughout her life, her burial could not take place until the Hamiltons had "taken upon themselves to discharge her debts, amounting to near £5000. Finally she was buried in the Hamilton vault at Bromley in Kent, with great funeral pomp the lady having expressed an earnest wish to be buried in a manner agreeable to her rank."[27]

Lord Derby had brought the news of his wife's death to Drury Lane on the day after. Learning that the long years of waiting were over put Elizabeth into such a state of nervous shock that she was quite unable to act that night.

The situation gave full rein to the caricaturists. One by Gillray called "Contemplations upon a Coronet" was unkind though clever and amsuing. Bearing the words, "A Coronet! O bless my sweet little heart. Ah! It must be mine, now there's nobody left in the way . . ." Elizabeth is shown sitting at her dressing-table, looking at a candlestick which has Lord Derby's head surmounted by a crimson and gold coronet on the top. In the bottom left-hand corner are the words "Tabby's Farewell to the Green-Room".[28] A different copy bears the words, "From Stocking-Lane to Derbyshire Peak". Such was the rather venomous ridicule Elizabeth had to put up with. The Dance of Death was particularly obnoxious. This shows Elizabeth and Lord Derby together in frantic exultation, dancing from right to left, his right arm round her waist, his left arm raised looking up at her. Her left leg is indecorously raised and a barking dog runs between the couple. The end of a coffin lid is open, showing the head of the first Lady Derby.[29]

The path to the altar was clear and as soon as he could, Lord Derby went to claim Elizabeth's hand. They arranged that she should take her leave of the stage "as soon as her spirits were equal to the effort." But what was clear to them privately was not clear to the public and questions were being asked. Now that he was free, was Lord Derby going to marry Elizabeth? Was he as much in love with her as ever or had his ardour cooled? Some said one thing and some the other and at the London Club, Whites, the betting was high as to the outcome. Rumour again had it that Lord Stanley – now 22 – would like to supplant his father. He escorted Elizabeth to and from the theatre every night during his father's widowerhood and this gave them the idea. But it was all nonsense. Malicious fingers were pointing at him because, when all was said and done, it was his own mother who had died.

In fact he was paying high tribute to Elizabeth, showing the world how happy he was to take care of her for his father – after all, she had been sweet and kind to him for nearly twenty years as his own mother had run away and left him.

Boaden settled the speculation. He had a foreboding, and then it was fulfilled, " . . . a stroke as of death was at hand, the sudden announcement of Miss Farren's retirement from the stage." Elizabeth would make her farewell on April 8th; what was of even more importance, Lord Derby announced "his intention to Miss Farren of elevating her speedily to a coronet."[30]

However high her star had shone in the theatrical firmament, Elizabeth had never lessened in her zeal for her profession nor slackened in the hard work necessary to keep up her high standard of performance. During the few days before her retirement she played:-

Violante in *The Wonder* on March 30th
Maria in *The Citizen* on April 1st
Estifania in *Rule a Wife and Have a Wife* on April 3rd
Susan in *The Follies of the Day* on April 4th
Bizarre in *The Inconstant* on April 6th

Quite a marathon, even for such an experienced actress as herself. How many actresses of her age could have performed such a number of parts in so short a space of time? And she only allowed herself one free evening before her farewell which she would make as Lady Teazle in *The School for Scandal*, a part she had played for the last fifteen years. " . . . so completely did she make the character of Lady Teazle her own notwithstanding the fact she had transformed Sheridan's less refined heroine into a fine Lady of her own time. Her fascinating performance of it almost obliterated the original representatoin of the part" wrote Mrs Mathews to which she added, "others played it with an insuperable rusticity and air of manners."[31]

Michael Kelly was at Drury Lane on April 8th, 1797, and commented:-

The theatre on the occasion was crowded to the ceiling, and the applause she received were as warm as she deserved. Her demeanour in the theatre was all affability and good nature: and in every action she was ever kind and lady-like. Lady Teazle, and other characters of high life she pourtrayed [sic] with all the vivid colouring of truth.[32]

The London Chronicle said:-

The public admiration of Miss Farren's talents, unrivalled as they have been for many years, in the representation of elegant and fashionable manners, and the general regret of her final secession from the stage, combined to attract to Drury Lane Theatre on Saturday a most brilliant and overflowing house.

Though no notice was given in the bills of the day she intended to close her career with her admirable performance of Lady Teazle in *The School for Scandal*, yet the press was so great in every part of the house to witness the last display of this accomplished actress, that it was impossible to procure a place for a considerable time before the curtain was drawn up, and several persons were much hurt in attempting to get to their boxes. Outside the house, several carriages were broken.[33]

Lord Derby reached his box safely and was received with the loudest acclamations; 3656 people were in the theatre – eleven more than it held officially. Except for a benefit night, the receipts at the box-office – £728 odd – were higher than ever before since the opening in 1794 and remained the record until its destruction by fire in 1800.

Described as "an elegant combination of taste and richness" – gold embroidery on a *coquelicote* (poppy-red) ground, Elizabeth looked breathtakingly beautiful and was greeted with several minutes of loud applause which "shewed the opinion the Public entertained of her eminent talents, and the sincere regret at the approaching chasm!"[34]

An eye-witness of the performance wrote, "Towards the conclusion of the play Miss Farren appeared much affected, and received much support from Mr King [Sir Peter Teazle] and Mr Wroughton [Manager of Drury Lane since September 1796]. The fall of the curtain was greeted with much applause for the loss of such an actress in the zenith of her charms and whilst her dramatic reputation was higher than ever."[35]

Such tumultuous applause had not been heard at Drury Lane before and it was accompanied by the universal waving of hats and handkerchiefs. What had tipped the scales on the side of tears for Elizabeth was when she said, ' . . . and inform them, that Lady Teazle, licentiate, begs leave to return the diploma they granted her, as she leaves off practice, and kills characters no more.'[36] As Boaden put it, "the application of familiar sentences to her own situation" was too much for her.

Having regained her equilibrium, Elizabeth curtsied to the right, to the left and to the centre. Then Mr Wroughton came forward and addressed the audience with these lines, written by Sheridan during the performance for the occasion.

But ah! this night adieu the mirthful mien,

When Mirth's lov'd fav'rite quits the Mimic scene!
Startled Thalia would assent refuse
But Truth and Virtue sued, and won the Muse
Aw'd by sensations it could ill express
Tho' mute the tongue, the bosom feel not less:
Her speech your kind indulgence oft has known,
Be to her Silence now that kindness shown;
Ne'er from her mind th'endear's record will part
But live the prowdest [sic] feeling of her grateful heart.[37]

"There were the most reiterated plaudits ever heard within the walls of a theatre," and Elizabeth made her way back-stage where there was a sequel to her previous allusion to Miss Mellon's light-heartedness.

The warm-hearted Harriot was crying in the wings in sympathy with the distress of her idol and as Elizabeth was assisted to a sofa, she followed. Seeing that Harriot was crying, she smiled at her kindly as she said, 'So there is a way to cloud even *your* enviable spirits.'[38]

Elizabeth rested a short time and then faced the ordeal of her final farewells to her colleagues; on entering the green-room she was met with a tremendous ovation from them. All were sad to see her go. Even at such a moment, Elizabeth remembered a small boy.

Every important actress was allotted a page-boy between five and nine years old to be at her beck and call as soon as she was dressed and ready for her part. As a farewell tip, Elizabeth gave her little page half-a-crown. If this is thought to be a pinch-penny amount the difference in the value of money between then and now should be remembered, taking into account that it was the very sum Gibson had given Elizabeth's father, "Lest peradventure thou shouldst lack the wherewithal to answer for a bed and supper." In the same context, nine shillings tip for Elizabeth's dresser represented a whole weeks wages so it was ample. Some years earlier, Boswell had said that thirty pounds a year was sufficient to enable a man to live in London for a year. Mrs Inchbald paid ten shillings a week for her lodgings in London at this time and when she dispensed with her sitting-room, the amount was reduced to six shillings and sixpence. Lodging in a garret cost 18 pence a week, a plain dinner sixpence and bread-and-milk, one penny.

Many actresses were over liberal in their tipping but they were invariably in debt. Not so Elizabeth, who paid her way without owing and she would also put her hand in her pocket when the need arose. Few other actors or actresses would have given £50 to the widow and children of a poor actor, but this was the sum Elizabeth gave promptly and gladly. She was always generous and settled "an annuity on her Mother."[39]

Tips and farewells over and done with, Elizabeth was again near fainting when the moment to leave the theatre arrived and she was half-carried to her coach by her devoted future step-son, Lord Stanley.

The newpapers were loud in their lamentations for the loss to the stage; "we have barely room to lament with the Public the irreparable loss which the stage has sustained by the retirement of this admirable actress"[40]wrote the Oracle. Boaden who had complimented her for her "sparkling captivations"[41]and "the innate delicacy with which she slurred many a risky passage in the old dramatists" now felt that "this theatrical demise absolutely produced the degeneracy of comedy into farce."[42]

"Since the first opening of Drury Lane, it has never been so full as it was on Saturday night." wrote Billinger's Liverpool Advertiser & Marriage Intelligence and included the explanatory sentence – as if the whole world didn't know – "Miss Farren made her final curtsey being about to take a more elevated cast of character on the great stage of life."

The longest comment came in the Monthly Mirror, a tiny paper, eight inches by five inches with very small print. It set out "to convey to posterity some stronger and more decisive memorial" to Elizabeth's excellencies than "the perishing columns" of the ordinary newspaper, "while our recollection of them is perfect."[43]

Rightly the article pointed out that Elizabeth was not faultless "but her merits were transcendant over her failings which were trivial," that she was an actress of "the first merit . . . in the path of elegant comedy she had no superior." Continuing that the preference for Mrs Abington by some was "by no means just". After extolling her personal charms came a long list of Elizabeth's talents and the writer added, "a rarer combination of nature and art has not been known. She possesses ease, vivacity, spirit and humour and her performances are so little injured by effort that we have often experienced the delusion of the senses, and imagined what in the theatre it is so difficult to imagine, the scene of action to be identified, and Miss Farren really the character which she is only attempting to sustain. We cannot admit the supposition ever, that St James's ever displayed superior evidence of fine breeding than Miss Farren has often done in her own person." He goes on to say that he has "every reason to believe that she will carry more of polished life *into* the drawing-room, than many ladies of quality, after an attendance of many years, have made shift to bring out of it". The article concludes:-

That another actress of equal merit will shortly supply the place her secession has left vacant, we have no hope: but tho we must regret her retirement, we cannot lament the occasion of it: it is meet that virtue and talent should be thus rewarded, and the stage, by her promotion to the peerage, will gain in ultimate respectability what it may lose in immediate consequence.[44]

A few days after her retirement came a paragraph as follows:-

In mentioning the expected marriage of Miss Farren with the Earl of Derby, it has been stated in some public prints, *and truly*, that the last female raised from the stage to a Coronet was Miss FENTON, who married the Duke of BOLTON.

But there is a marked difference in the two cases; that even calumny has never dared to cast the slightest imputation on Miss FARREN'S character, whereas Miss LAVINIA FENTON, the original Polly Peachum of Gay's Beggar's Opera lived several years with Charles the Third Duke of Bolton, after which he certainly did marry her.[45]

About four months before Elizabeth's retirement, Farington referred to Sheridan's habit of deferring players' payment as "unprincipled", and Lord Derby presented himself at Drury Lane, shortly after Elizabeth's farewell, seeking her arrears. He was reported to have said he would not stir from the theatre without the money but the charming, witty Sheridan placated him with an elegant compliment. "This is too bad, You have taken from us the brightest jewel in the world, and now you quarrel about a little dust she leaves behind her." This letter from Elizabeth to Sheridan had evidently had no effect. It is undated but must have been written not long before April 8th, 1797.

> Miss Farren's Compts to Mr Sheridan and informs him She cannot think of playing to night till he has given an order for their returning the money She has had so unjustly stopt [sic] from *her* this day for not attending rehearsals. She comes to night at the danger of her life has been extremely ill the whole week and inclind [sic] as She allways [sic] is to do her best to serve the Managers She cannot but look on their behaviour as the greatest instance of cruelty and contempt she ever knew.[46]

Why should Elizabeth think she should be an exception to the rule of levying fines on players for non-attendance at rehearsals? All the same, even several fines could hardly cancel out her salary of £18 a week.

Writing of the "considerable alterations" at Drury Lane in the summer recess of 1797/98, Elizabeth's admirer, John Adolphus said,

> . . . but the great and distinguishing loss which the company sustained occurred on 8th April, when Miss Farren, after performing the part of Lady Teazle with her accustomed and acknowledged excellence, bade adieu to the theatre. She did not speak her farewell; Wroughton uttered a short address. Miss Farren, having curtsied to all parts of the house, left a void which has never been adequately filled. Her graceful person, elegant address, and exquisite representation of ladies of quality, could be seen and felt by all of every class; but it required closer observation to discern that excellence which gave to her performance its highest charm – a delicate genuine, impressive sensibility, which reached the heart of a process no less certain than that by which her other powers effected the impression on her fancy and judgment. She retired from the simulated to the real dignity; being immediately, but not unexpectedly, elevated by marriage to the Earl of Derby, to the rank of Countess.[47]

It is written that "popular applause is lighter than a feather or a bubble and less substantial than a dream" – but in Elizabeth's case, it had meant something. Democrat that she was, she must have appreciated her place in the hearts of the populace. Also she must have been pleased when that splendid provincial theatre manager, Tate Wilkinson wrote:-

> such fashion, ease, pleasantry and elegance in the Captivating coquette and Lady of fashion all conjoined as when I view the alluring, the entertaining, the all-acomplished Miss Farren – good actresses may put in their claims, but that face, with the domains [sic] that adjacent lie – in short, the tout *ensemble* is not to be equalled.[48]

After Elizabeth's retirement, Mrs Jordan seized her chance and lost

no time in introducing herself where she judged it would do most good
– to James Boaden. "The retirement of Miss Farren led her to think of
extending her range of Characters."[49]Doubtless she envisaged being
able to remedy the loss wept over by Boaden but he said, "the stage
lost its only woman of fashion. I say its *Only* Woman of Fashion."[50]

There was no hypocrisy over the date of Elizabeth's marriage; no
respect was pretended where none was felt – or due.

> Miss Farren is to play The Wedding Day on Monday next.
> A Special Licence to that effect was taken out on Tuesday.
> The Matrimonial Dress is of superb style. Mr and Mrs
> Knight, who will then be nearly related to the Earl of
> Derby, will it is thought, also quit the stage:[51] [They did
> not].

Monday was April 17th but in the event, the wedding was postponed
for a fortnight. Whigs drank a lot of port and Lord Derby had a
sharp attack of gout.

Mrs Piozzi wrote on April the 26th, "Miss Farren is bride-expectant
and everybody appears to applaud Lord Derby's choice:"[52] five days
later on May Day, Monday May 1st, Lord Derby and Elizabeth were
married.

> On Monday last, at his home in Grosvenor Square, by
> Special Licence, by Reverend John Hornby, vicar of
> Winnick, the Right Honourable the Earl of Derby to
> Miss Farren of Green Street Grosvenor Square; after
> which they set off for the Oaks.[53]

Elizabeth's mother and her sister, Peggy Knight, were witnesses and
in the register the name was correctly spelt Farr*an*.

On the night of the wedding, Elizabeth's friend Mrs Siddons, took
her benefit in Lillo's *Fatal Curiosiity* and "at the conclusion of the
evening's entertainment, forth came the Queen of Tears to weep over
the loss of Comedy."

166

Boaden continued:-

It well became such a woman as Mrs Siddons to notice the loss with a kind wish for the future happiness of her amiable sister of the scene. Accordingly, after a most affecting performance by Kemble and herself of Lillo's soul-harrowing *Fatal Curiosity*, to which *The Deuce is in Him* was the farce, she thus noticed that her friend on that day became Lady Derby.

Our Comic Muse, too, lighter topics lending,
Proves that in marriage was her natural ending:
While grateful for those smiles she made us gay,
Each kindest wish attends her wedding-day.
And sure, such talents, honours, shar'd between 'em
If 'tis not happy, why the deuce is in 'em.[54]

The papers remarked next day that the words "were a poor compliment to Miss Farren and a pointed attack on Mrs Jordan." The verse came from Mrs Piozzi's pen, "Miss Farren has married Lord Derby at last, and She is well-liked and happy they tell me. I wrote some lines for Mrs Siddons's Leavetaking, and mentioned her good Fortune but I can't remember ye lines *and* I took no copy."[54]

Of the many comments on the marriage, Boaden's is the most apt and welcome. "Her dwelling-house has long been graced by the portraits of the Derby family and The Union was not less desired than expected by the children of the first marriage."[55]

There was a curiosity amongst the wedding-presents, an allegorical poem of forty-nine verses.

A Legend, Presented on their marriage to the Right Honourable The Earl of Derby and Countess of Derby. Printed by the Author, Price 6d.

Here is the first verse, and the last two lines.

> To legend the Muse must apply for resource,
> When we live in an age so refin'd
> That ecomium direct may abate of its force
> By oppressing the delicate mind.

x x x

> May Reason's still voice speak this truth in your heart
> That Religion's the cement of love.

Marriage for love was almost unheard of at the time, and so was a virtuous actress. Elizabeth was not the first actress to marry into the nobility but she had the distinction of being the first to do so without any scandal. Furthermore, Lord Derby was reputed to be the richest peer in England – and also the ugliest! The marriage led to a spate of caricatures, all of them outstripped by James Gillray's "The Marriage of Cupid and Psyche." This is a brilliant travesty of the first century Roman cameo called "The Marlborough Gem" now in the Museum of Fine Arts, Boston, Mass.

Two comments with different slants will not come amiss here:-

> When Miss Farren really in private life assumed the dignity of her present rank, the elevation was deemed neither abrupt or surprising, but rather as if Lady Emily Gayville in The Heiress had obtained the superior title of Countess of Derby.[56]

The next one reminds the public of Elizabeth's moral standards:

> Every night of her performances speaks her praises too well for us to attempt the eulogium of Miss Farren. She came out as Miss Hardcastle; her sensibility, action and delivery, soon raised her to the utmost height of reputation; – it is since making the above observations that this Lady is become Countess of Derby, a proof that virtue

joined to talent, is in this country held equal in consideration to any rank or condition.[57]

The scurrilous anonymous writer, Petronius Arbiter was one who made great play with the shortness of Lord Derby's and Elizabeth's honeymoon of only four days at The Oaks. "They found not in the joys of love and solitude enough to make then forget the Dissipations of the Town . . . "[58]Perhaps they were impatient to return to London and the "remarkable domed twin bed in the round-toped [sic] alcove" which Adam had created in the first-floor bedchamber at Derby House!

Even when they were back, Arbiter says, "for the first month, they could not find their way to the Hymenal Bed *before* Four O'Clock *each morning!*" He hints that Lord Derby lacked the "Capacities and Energies" for the "Prime Bliss of the Married State." As usual, Arbiter was inaccurate.

1. Mathews, Charles. Memoirs 1839 Vol.i
2. Joseph Farran's portrait by Wm. Collyer, a pupil of Sir T. Lawrence, is also in the United States
3. Mathews. op.cit. p.101
4. Ibid p.102
5. Ibid p.107
6. Ibid p.114
7. Ibid Vol.iii
8. Dublin Evening Post July 5.1794
9. Walpole to Mary Berry. Sept.27th 1794
10. The Times Oct. 2nd 1794
11. Lawrence,W.J. Dr op.cit. p.97
12. Hazlitt, Wm. Essays on the Drama 1820. p.49
13. Baron-Wilson, op.cit. p.191
14. Walpole, Toynbee. op.cit. Vol.15 No.2896
15. Mrs Mathews. Ennobled Actresses p.43
16. Waldron, F.G. Candid and Impartial Strictures on the Performances 1795. p.170
17. Bellamy, Th. The London Theatres. 1795 Vol.ii
18. Farington, Joseph. Diaries of. Vol.13 p.803, from the typed copy of the Farington Diaries, the originals of which are in the Royal Library, Windsor Castle.
19. Gore's General Advertiser Aug.26th 1796
20. Farington, as n.18
21. Boaden. Life of Mrs Jordan 1831 p.315
22. Baron-Wilson. op.cit p.190
23. Stephens, F G. Catalogue of Political & Personal Satires B.M. No. 7736 Vol.vi. No.7736
24. Shakespeare, Wm, Hamlet. Act III, Scene I.
25. Baron-Wilson. op.cit. Vol.i p.192
26. Monthly Mirror. Nov.1796

27. Gentlemen's Magazine. Jan-June 1797

28. Stephens. op.cit. Vol.vii. No.9074

29. Ibid. No.9075

30. Boaden, Jordan Vol.i. p.319

31. Mathews, Mrs. op.cit. p.48

32. Kelly, Michael. Reminiscences. 1826 p.340

33. London Chronicle April 8th-11th 1797

34. Ibid

35. Morning Chronicle April 1829

36. Sheridan, R.B. The School for Scandal. Last scene.

37. Morning Herald 12th April 1797

38. Baron-Wilson. op.cit. p.216

39. Lewes, Chas. Lee. op.cit. Memoirs 1805 Vol.ii. p.2

40. The Oracle & Public Advertiser, April 10th 1797

41. Boaden, Siddons p.343

42. Ibid. p.318

43. Monthly Mirror, April 1797

44. Ibid.

45. The Oracle & Public Advertiser, April 10th 1797

46. By kind permission of the Governors of Harrow School

47. Adolphus, op.cit. p.387

48. Wilkinson. Wandering Patentee

49. Boaden, Jordan p.322

50. Ibid p.320

51. The Oracle, April 8th 1797

52. Piozzi, Thraliana, Intimate Letters of, p.972, April 26, 1797

53. Billinger's Liverpool Advertiser

54. Piozzi, Thraliana op.cit

55. Boaden, Life of J.P. 1827 2 vols. vol.iii. p.196

56. Adolphus, op.cit.

57. Waldron. A Compendium History of the Theatre 1797. The Curtain.

58. Post Extension to Memoirs of the present Countess of Derby Petronius Arbiter. 5th edition. p.31

Chapter Eleven

Cast in her final rôle as the Countess of Derby, Elizabeth played it with customary grace and skill. Her marriage did not separate her from her devoted mother who was given her own apartments in Derby House and nearly always accompanied the couple either to Knowsley or to The Oaks in Surrey. The annuity given by Elizabeth was probably settled on her mother after her marriage.

Two anonymous sketches of Elizabeth's life were written in 1797, the year of her marriage. *The Memoirs of the Present Countess of Derby [late Miss Farren]* by "Petronius Arbiter" was the first. The writer claimed his pseudonym was the real name of his "Great Ancestor and namesake who wrote in the debauched reign of Nero and enjoyed all the luxuries of a Palace while I starve in a garret."[1] Here then, he gives his reason for writing this scurrilous and untrue account of Elizabeth's background and her life, purporting to be her memoirs. For financial gain he sought to satisfy the avid, insatiable appetite and curiosity of the public for the intimate details of the private lives of those in the limelight.

It was as much to the advantage of his story that he disparaged Elizabeth's true background as it was to make untrue statements such as that she had been a housemaid and "trundled a mop in Bath." He dwelt on the extreme poverty through which the family had passed after the death of George Farran but for all his efforts, he was quite unable to point a finger at Elizabeth's morals and had to rest on Ugo Foscolo's observation, "The English are a humane people, but will have nothing to do with one who wants bread . . . Poverty is a disgrace that no merit can wipe off. Indigence would render Homer despicable in their eyes."[2]

The real name of Petronius Arbiter is said to have been John Williamson and Elizabeth was by no means the only butt of his barbs; he made his livelihood out of "satirising the best Characters in the Kingdom."[3]

Fast on Arbiter's heels came "The Testimony of Truth to Exalted Merit in Refutation of Scandalous Libel" which was also anonymous and tore Arbiter to shreds. It has been ascribed to R. B. Sheridan and could well have been by him as he was one of Elizabeth's staunch supporters and friends. The author was very much up in arms on her behalf and wrote, "Though the reputation of the exalted person to whom this tribute is offered can require no defence, the impudent assertions of a lying slanderer ought to be refuted."[4]

Six years after these two, in 1805, Lee Lewes poured contempt on "the falsifications" which had been published about the Farran family. He is one of the few who contradicts statements that George Farran came from Cork, giving the correct native city of the family as Dublin. Lewes quotes Henry Fielding in Tom Jones, "that it is necessary for an author to have some knowledge of his subject before he sits down to write it. This axiom I may truly say has been totally neglected by the historians who have so daringly palmed upon the public the spurious accounts of the Farrens . . . surreptitious memoirs by misinformed biographers." He continues that many of his readers "have been misled by seeing very fallacious accounts of the Farren family, which for what purpose I cannot tell, have been published in many of our Monthly Magazines." Of Elizabeth he wrote, "May Miss Farren long live the pattern of Virtue."[5]

The Times announced a week after her marriage, "Lady Derby will be shortly introduced at Court." Then, on 11th May:-

The Queen will have a Drawing-room this day, at which the Prince of Wirtemberg [sic] will be present. The Countess of Derby will be presented[7]

And on the following day, May 12th:-

Yesterday there was a very crowded Drawing-room at St James's. The Countess of Harcourt attended the Queen,

173

Lady C. Belayse the Princesses and the Countess of Cholmondeley the Princess of Wales.[8]

The list of presentations was headed by Elizabeth's name and hers was the only dress described. With her impeccable taste, she was dressed simply but perfectly for the occasion.

The Countess of Derby was yesterday dressed very plain, and almost unornamented; but it was of the neatest kind, all white.[9]

A contemporary account elaborates on her attire in saying that her dress was of "Chamberry gauze, and white bugles, and her head ornamented only with a small white feather and spray and a narrow bandeau of white bugles on her hair, which was lightly powdered." Elizabeth was introduced at Court by Lady Celia Johnston.[10]The same account states that the ceremonial was "conducted on the part of the Countess, with an elegance of demeanour equally free from affectation and embarrassment. After the Queen had conversed with her some time and retired, she received marked attention of the principal nobility etc., present." She had gone to Court "in the plain family coach, attended by two footmen in their usual liveries, the whole appearance was devoid of ostentation, or parade."[11]Lord Derby was dressed in mourning!

Queen Charlotte and Elizabeth were not strangers having met at Richmond House and elsewhere on numerous occasions, so one would have thought Elizabeth would have taken the presentation ceremony in her stride, but this was not the case. It is further proof of how unspoilt she was that an eye-witness reported that she was nervous. This was Samuel Lysons who said 'she appeared a little confused. The King, in addressing Her, said He hoped she wd acquit Herself with the same propriety in Her new as in her late situation.'[12]Lady Gage who was there too said 'when Lady Derby was presented, the Queen *advanced* to Her, which is a great compliment.'[13]It was also reported that Elizabeth "was singled out by Her Majesty who conversed with her for some time in the Circle." Known for her lively conversation and wit, Elizabeth may well have made this remark at her presentation, 'that the most blissful moment of my life was appearing before Your Majesty in a new charcter'.[14]

The Court was most fastidious and Queen Charlotte as strait-laced as could be. She had never allowed the first Countess of Derby to come to Court after she had left Lord Derby. Now the Royal Family plainly approved of Elizabeth and by paying marked attention to her, Queen Charlotte proved beyond doubt – if further proof be needed – that she had at no time been Lord Derby's mistress.

> Queen Charlotte, the most rigid discriminator of female worth, received her with special marks of recognisance, and it must be regarded as a Peculiar Honour conferred for the blamelessness of her professional life, that she was selected to make one in the procession at the marriage of the Princess Royal.[15]

This was a signal favour. Those who were not invited to walk in the Royal procession were asked to attend a special Drawing-room after the service. Elizabeth would attend this in any case on account of her rank, but to "make one in the procession", that was something very special.

There is an amusing story about one of the Princess Royal's wedding presents:-

> Forster, the Court jeweller, had almost completed a valuable ring of thirty diamonds, when a hen got into the workshop, picked out the diamonds one by one, and swallowed them. Caught in the act of swallowing the last, the hen was killed immediately. All the stones were removed from its gizzard and the ring duly completed in time to present to the Princess Royal.[16]

The match between the thirty-eight year old Princess Royal who was enormously fat, and the Hereditary Prince (later King) of Wirtemberg, was hardly love's young dream. Apart from the bride's unprepossessing appearance, it was rumoured that her elderly bridegroom's first wife was still alive. Queen Charlotte had a poor opinion of her eldest daughter's taste in clothes and made much of her trousseau – and her wedding-dress – herself.

The Grand Gala Day, the 18th May, was fine, "all the avenues leading to St James's Palace were crouded [sic] at an early hour . . ." Those in the Royal procession – including Elizabeth – waited in the Great Council Chamber, moving off when they were joined by the King and Queen. "Her Royal Highness the Bride never looked to so much advantage," said one onlooker – strange when another said, "the Bride had jaundice." The Princess Augusta talked with Fanny Burney (Madame D'Arblay) about her sister's wedding.

> She, (Princess Augusta) gave me some account of the ceremony; and when I told her I had heard that her Royal Highness the Bride had never looked so lovely, she confirmed the praise warmly, but laughingly added, 'Twas the Queen dressed her! You know what a figure she used to make of herself, with her odd manner of dressing herself'; but mamma said, "Now really Princess Royal, this one time is the last, and I cannot suffer you to make such a quiz of yourself; so I will really have you dressed properly." And indeed the Queen was quite right, for everybody said she had never looked so well in her life.[17]

After the ceremony, Elizabeth and the others guests repaired to the Great Drawing-Room where the King and Queen were ensconced under a canopy to receive the many congratulations on their daughter's marriage. Joseph Farington wrote in his diary, "Princess Royal's marriage today. Pall Mall full of Coaches this afternoon of Company at Court to congratulate."[18]

Newspaper reports gave the names of Royalty who attended the "Select Drawing-Room" next day. Only four other names were given.

"The Duchess of Gordon, Countesses Derby and Jersey and Lady A Carpenter were among the company." Other than those worn by Royalty, there was a short list of dresses, Elizabeth's coming after those of the Marchionesses of Hertford and Bute.

> *The Countess of Derby* was very elegantly dressed in a white crape [sic] petticoat, richly embroidered with small sprigs, over the right corner of which flowed two draperies, differently spangled, and ornamented with beautiful festoon borders in Silver Wheat-ears, and fancy sprigs; the pocket holes ornamented with rich cord and dress tassels, [sic] and silver flounce round the bottom; body and train of white and silver tissue and silver fringe.[19]

An elaborate description and rather hard to visualise! But could the "silver tissue" be the silver muslin her grateful cousin Charles Farran had sent from India?

After her marriage, Elizabeth gave a handsome present to a disappointed suitor. Let Mrs Papendiek take up the story.

> Miss Farren, the beautiful actress was wooed by both Lord Derby and Mr Archibald Seton. As is well known she chose the former. The tradition is that she sent the full-length portrait by Zoffany (as Hermione in *A Winter's Tale*) to the unsuccessful wooer, Mr Archibald Seton of Touch near Stirling. This gentleman never married but the portrait remained at Touch.[20]

Archibald Seton succeeded his mother as Laird of Touch; he was Governor of Penang. This century the portrait went through Agnew's salerooms and now hangs in the National Gallery of Victoria, Melbourne, Australia.

A portrait of the Twelfth Earl of Derby painted by Hoppner, hangs in the Committee corridor of the House of Commons. In 1797 Hoppner painted a portrait "which is said to represent the charming actress [Elizabeth] but this, from its general unlikeness to the approved

Farren type, is now suspect."[21]This portrait did not descend through the Stanley family but was bought by the then Earl of Derby, circa 1899.

Hoppner was acknowledged to be extremely jealous of Sir Thomas Lawrence and though it is sometimes said that artists did not pay much attention to the colour of eyes, if Hoppner sought to equal or rival Sir Thomas' beautiful full length of Elizabeth, it seems more than strange he gave her brown eyes – dark brown at that. Her arresting blue eyes were her most distinctive feature and are often mentioned by contemporaries.

   a) Her lustrous blue eyes.[22]
   b) Her eye is blue and penetrating.[23]
   c) Her eyes were blue.[24]
   d) Her merry blue eyes.[25]

And it will be remembered that Lawrence had a particular aptitude for painting eyes.

After becoming Countess of Derby compliments continued to flow:-

> In speaking of Miss Farren's marriage with the Earl of Derby, she [Princess Augusta] displayed that sweet mind which her state & station has so wholly escaped sullying; for far from expressing either resentment or derision at an actress being elevated to the rank of 2nd Countess of England, she told me, with an air of satisfaction, that she was informed she had behaved extremely well since her marriage, & done many generous & charitable actions.[26]

Another commentator wrote "in real dignity she conducted herself as elegantly deserving of admiration in the mimic scene". The following one was equally admiring but with a different slant, "The profession she has just quitted will acquire a respectabilty; rank alone, unsupported by real worth, would serve to make it infamous rather than illustrious."

Seeing the life she led, perhaps Elizabeth might have been forgiven, had she not been domesticated but the reverse was the case and she made as excellent a wife as anyone could have wished. Although only a few weeks off her thirty-eighth birthday at her marriage, she bore her lord four children in as many years and, what is more, kept her elegant sylph-like figure, weighing only nine stone, twelve pounds after the fourth.[27]

She had her first baby in March 1798, ten months after marrying Lord Derby. So much for the aspersions cast on his virility and the caricature published about the time of their marriage! This shows Lord Derby and Elizabeth smoking long pipes, but no smoke issues from Lord Derby's pipe. She touches his clumsy shoe with the toe of her slipper saying. 'You have no Fire in your Pipe, my dear Derby', he answers, 'It has been out long ago, my lovey, but I like to whiff with an agreeable companion, what the children call make believe!'[28]

In that era it was common enough but somehow sadder for Lord Derby and Elizabeth that the seal of their love, a baby daughter, was still-born. Nothing daunted, she allowed little time to elapse before she tried again. Lucy Elizabeth was born on March 12, 1799, followed by James on March 9th 1800 and Mary-Margaret on March 23rd in 1801. All the children had the name Smith-Stanley as had Lord Derby, whose mother Lucy Smith, was her father's heiress. In his will, he stipulated that his sons-in-law must take his name. (Lord Derby's grandson, the Fourteenth Earl of Derby dropped Smith from his patronymic).

Evidence that Elizabeth was adept with her needle and made clothes for her babies is shown by the exquisitely embroidered fine lawn bonnet and shirt she made for one of them. On the shoulders of the shirt in the finest of work – so fine it is almost indiscernible to the naked eye – are the words:-

Dear Babe, fear God and keep his laws.

Miraculously the little garments are in pristine condition, carefully preserved and treasured by Elizabeth's descendants.

The deep devotion of Lord Stanley and his sister, Lady Charlotte Stanley, to their step-mother was unquestioned but no mention of the attitude of the youngest, Lady Elizabeth Henrietta Stanley has ever been found and Joseph Farington, in 1798, give the clue. He tells that Lord Derby had settled £7,000 on Lord Stanley and "he has given £28,000 to Lady Charlotte, £2,000 only to Lady Elizabeth, the latter the supposed daughter of the Duke of Dorset."[29]In the circumstances it is surprising that he gave her anything at all but he had a kind, warm nature and she had been brought up with his own children. She had already been married off to a Mr Stephen Cole in 1795. She could not have been more than sixteen then.

Farington's friend, Frank Jodrell told him that "he has been much with Lord Derby and speaks warmly of his good disposition . . . his circumstances are very flourishing. He has £30,000 a year in improving condition and makes purchases. He is an excellent Lord Lieutenant, never allows business to stand still, answers letter by return of post. Lady Derby pleases people by her attentions. She is to be a great . . . Occonomist [sic]."[30] Her early years had laid the foundation for that.

Lord Derby was, as a leading Whig, prominent in the political life of the country. Until he succeeded his grandfather, the Eleventh Earl, he served in the House of Commons. When he became the Twelfth Earl, he served in the House of Lords for the rest of his life. He was intensely loyal and a Privy Councillor. In addition, he made an excellent Lord Lieutenant of Lancashire. Very popular with the people there he was returned to Parliament with a large majority at every election while he was in the Commons.

Only just over a year after their own marriage, Elizabeth and Lord Derby had the pleasure of the marriage of Lord Stanley to his cousin, Margaret Hornby, the daughter of his Aunt Lucy. He was only twenty-three but "he was so deaf as to be obliged to use a Trumpet."[31]Their first child, Edward Geoffrey, was born at Knowsley a few months after Elizabeth's daughter, Lucy Elizabeth making her a mother and a step-grandmother at a stroke so to speak. Much of their time was spent by the Derbys at beautiful Knowsley as Mrs Mathews tells:

"the greater portion of the time the noble pair spent annually at their country seat in calm and rational enjoyment; and it may be added, without a *quibble*, that they furnished in their inseparable union of sentiment, tastes and pursuits, a high-life illustration of Darby and Joan, giving the tenantry and neighbouring poor cause to bless the day that *conducted this peerless actress* to the honour of a peerage."[32]

Knowsley, about eight miles from Liverpool, stood in an extensive park with two lakes, one three miles wide in part, and many beautiful trees, principally oak. It had come to the Stanleys by the marriage of Sir John Stanley with Isabella de Lathom in 1385. Their great-grandson was created Earl of Derby for his services at the Battle of Bosworth Field (1485) through which the throne of England was secured for Henry VII. The King's mother, Margaret Beaufort, became the Earl of Derby's second wife (and he her third husband). It is said that the Royal Apartments at Knowsley were built by the first Earl to welcome his Royal stepson on his first visit.

The journey from London to Knowsley in Elizabeth's day took several days. Until the advent of John Macadam (post 1815) the roads were appalling. Although the Derbys could afford the best coaches that money could buy, the journey was thoroughly uncomfortable. In the last half of the eighteenth century English coachbuilding was paramount and there was a large export market, but early in the next century "the cost had so much increased . . . that foreign nations prefer to deal with manufacturers who can give them a vehicle which, to the eye, appears as good as our own, and in colours and finish more to their taste, whilst the price is from 10 to 30 persent [sic] less than a British carriage." Even then, England was pricing herself out of foreign markets.[33]

Through the ages Knowsley held a great reputation for hospitality though after the third Earl died in 1572, "the glory of hospitality seemed to fall asleep." It had certainly reawakened. Lord Derby loved to fill the house and was the life and soul of any party while Elizabeth made the perfect châtelaine. In her day, there were never less than forty guests from June to November and during the shooting season, Lord Derby had a strict rule that no gun might bag more than five brace of partridge in the morning so as to ensure good sport for the ladies to watch in the afternoon. The luncheon table on Mondays was always set for one hundred; and sundry were welcome.

The estate was self-supporting. Meat, poultry, game, vegetables and fruit came off the land. Butter was churned in an exquisite dairy designed by Robert Adam. According to the Liverpool Chronicle in 1813, during September 1812 the following were consumed in the month:-

4,995 lbs beef; 3224 lbs mutton; 5,320 quarts ale; 6,440 quarts of beer.[34]

It should be remembered that guests brought their children, servants, coaches, horses and grooms as well as coachmen, and they all had to be accommodated and fed.

At Knowsley Lord Derby and Elizabeth were surrounded by beauty. The house was screened by trees from the road and it had a pleasing symmetry, well set-off by formal gardens and the park. Indoors, the beauties included an outstanding collection of paintings made by the Tenth Earl with works by Vandyck, Rubens, Veronese and many others. Lord Derby, a collector himself, had added his own choice. Amongst them were a rare landscape by the French painter, Nicholas Poussin, painted in 1648 and entitled, "Landscape with the Gathering of the Ashes of Phocion". Acquired by Lord Derby between 1776 and 1782, it was sold by the Trustees of Lord Derby's Heirloom Settlement to the Walker Gallery in Liverpool for £1,150,000 in 1984. The price sets the seal on Lord Derby's taste.[35]

The Knowsley library was stocked with beautiful books, many bought by the Derbys at the sale of the effects of their great friend Horace Walpole, who died a few weeks before their marriage. They also acquired a large Chinese bowl of blue and white porcelain on an ebony stand known as "The Strawberry Hill bowl", (the name of Horace Walpole's House at Twickenham). Walpole's favourite cat was drowned trying to catch the goldfish in it and Thomas Gray, his friend from Eton days, wrote an ode on the episode which includes these lines:-

> She stretched in vain to reach the prize
> What female heart can gold despise?
> What cat's averse to fish?[36]

Had Ireland been in a more settled state in 1799, Elizabeth could have had the opportunity of returning some of the generous hospitality of Charles Farran in Dublin. As it was, he wrote to say he could not come, "particularly until we know the Destination of the French Fleet, as should it be bound for this unhappy Country as I may call it . . . I coud [sic] not think of leaving the Girls with a protector tho' I was ever so much inclind [sic] to pay a visit...'[37]Rathgar, Charles' estate south of Dublin, was very isolated and his carter had been murdered the year before. When the culprits were taken past the scene of their crime on the way to the gallows, six months later, they were asked why they had murdered the man and replied, 'because he was an Orangeman.'[38]

Seven years before Charles Farran wrote that letter, Lord Cloncurry was writing, "this Orange Society is a sign of the times its formation marks the revival of anti-Roman Catholic feeling among Protestants; the Roman Catholics are favourable to the French Revolution which had made an attack on property, the Ascendancy is founded on property . . . the Roman Catholics are in league with France and she is ready to swallow Europe." In October 1792 Lord Westmoreland wrote to Pitt. "It is very extraordinary but I believe the two sects of Irish hate and fear each other as much as they did one hundred years ago . . . "[39]

Quite apart from the political situation in Ireland, Charles would be loath to leave his daughters for another reason – forcible abduction of girls of good family was rife at that time. Abduction clubs existed which concentrated on kidnapping daughters of wealthy fathers. Charles's salary as Deputy Clerk of the Pleas was worth the very high sum of £5,270.5s.ll½d. and he continued in the post until his death, aged 85. Although he lived for ten years after he wrote that letter, it is probable that he and Elizabeth never met again. Charles junior in India wrote on a slip of paper, "My Dearly Beloved Father died on Xmas Day" (12808). He owned a good miniature of his father by John Comerford which his great-great grandson, Colonel Joseph William Farran, Secretary of the Cavalry Club, lent to the Victoria and Albert Museum. After his death in 1894 the Farrans neglected to reclaim the miniature which is always on display.

In November 1803, the Derbys had a problem, not unexpected, which led to gossip. At the Hoppners house, Farington learnt that Lady Charlotte Hornby "had gone from Her Husband to *his friend* Mr Taddy in the Temple, on Saturday last. Hornby came home to dinner at the usual hour – no Lady Charlotte, at Eleven o'clock she sent for her Maid – at 3 in the morning she was taken from Mr Taddy's but not home. Lord and Lady Derby sent for to the Oaks . . . so goes the story." [40] What had happened? Seemingly she was a chip off her own mother's block? She too had abandoned her baby son.

A month later she was still at Derby House with her father and Elizabeth, as much enamoured of Mr Taddy as ever. The outcome was settled when she died the following year.

The fashion then was to be weighed in public, at Number Three St James's Street, then a grocery shop. In 1765, the custom of weighing books was introduced and the Stanley book was begun by the Twelfth Earl of Derby.

There in 1803, Elizabeth's weight was recorded as nine stone twelve pounds. Lord Derby's weight is not known but James aged three, turned the scales at two stone five pounds. The scales used were those on which the groceries had been weighed. They are still in place in Berry Brothers and Rudd. Everyone of consequence in Elizabeth's day was weighed there – no hiding ladies' weights as today – except Charles James Fox and the Prince Regent. Perhaps because they were both so obese! It is hardly necessary to add that the name of Berry Brothers is still synonomous with fine wine the world over.[41]

Elizabeth's mother was taken ill at Derby House at the end of May 1803 and died in her own apartments there on June 5th. She was in her seventy-first year. The ideal relationship which existed between them is described by J. R. Broadbent.

> In obscurity and in affluence her amiable mother was her "guide, philosopher and friend." In the humble lodging and in the splendid salons where homage was paid to her beauty and genius by the noblest in the land, the influence of her mother was the same. They appeared to study each other's happiness so perfectly and with such ease and with such unrestrained action, as convinced every unprejudiced visitor or beholder that the most unlimited friendship prevailed between them, and that their sole contest was which should render the other happiest.[42]

How proud and happy Elizabeth's mother must have been of her daughter's success on the stage and as the Countess of Derby. What is more, she herself died secure in the devoted affection of her daughter and of her noble son-in-law who was exceedingly fond of her and happy to have her living with them. The next year, 1804, Elizabeth's sister died. Elizabeth was now the sole survivor of her family.

On 14th June 1803, the Manchester Mercury paid this charming tribute:

" . . . a lady whose many virtues and mild, affectionate and placid manners will make her death the subject of deep and lasting regret to all who had the pleasure of her acquaintance." [43]

Although she had left the stage eight years previously, Elizabeth was by no means forgotten. Lee Lewes wrote in highly complimentary terms in 1805 and Cumberland said in 1806, " . . . I cannot avoid to speak of one of the most elegant actresses that ever graced the stage". Then in 1808, Gilliland wrote in The Dramatic Mirror, "her elegant representations of Lady Teazle are still remembered with delight."

Chapter Eleven - Footnotes

1. Petronius Arbiter. (Anon) op.cit.
2. Vincent, C.R. Ugo Foscolo
3. T.O.T. p.6.
4. Ibid p.7.
5. Lewes op.cit. vol.ii p.2.
6. The Times, May 8th 1797.
7. The Times, May 11th 1787.
8. The Times, May 12th 1797.
9. Ibid.
10. Lady Henrietta-Cecilia Johnson, dau. of John West, 1st Earl of de la Warr.
11. Sporting Intelligence, May 1797
12. Farington, op.cit. vol.iii. p.1021.
13. Ibid. p.1025.
14. Ibid. p.1021
15. Galt, op.cit. p.233.
16. Fitzgerald, Percy. The Good Queen Charlotte. 1899, footnote p.224.
17. Burney, Fanny. (Mdme D'Arblay) The Journals and Letters of Fanny Burney, O.U.P. ed. Joyce Hemlow, 1972-1978 vol.iii p.295
18. Farington, op. cit. vol.iii. p.1020.
19. The True Briton, May 18th 1797.
20. Papendiek but quoted by Manners & Williamson in "Zoffany".
21. Lawrence, Dr. op.cit. p.100.
22. McDermott (undated Irish Newspaper).
23. Morning Chronicle.
24. D.N.B.
25. Stirling, M.A.W. The Hothams. 1918 vol.II. p.226.
26. Hemlow op. cit. vol.iv. Nov. 3rd 1797 p.23.
27. Berry Bros. & Rudd Magazine. "Number Three St James's Street". Spring 1978 p.II.

28. Stephens, op. cit. No. 9074.
29. Farington, op. cit. vol.ii. p.763.
30. Ibid. vol.iii. p.1331.
31. Ibid.
32. Mathews, Mrs. Tea Table Talk. p.50.
33. Thrupp, G.A. The History of Coaches 1877. p.66.
34. Liverpool Chronicle, Sept. 1813.
35. National Arts Collections Fund Report. 1985.
36. Gray, Thomas. Designs by Mr R. Bentley for 6 poems by. 1753. Ode 2.
37. Letter to his daughter Martha Farran (wife of his nephew) from Charles Farran senr. 28th May 1799.
38. Freeman's Journal, 1798.
39. Cloncurry, Lord. V.B. Lawless, Second Baron. Life & Times of Lord Cloncurry 1849.
40. Farington. op. cit. p.2442.
41. Note 27
42. Broadbent, J. R. Journal of the Hist. Soc. of Lanc. & Cheshire. Vol. LXI.
43. Manchester Mercury, June 14th 1803.

Chapter Twelve

Of the very many who were entertained at Knowsley was Thomas Creevey, a staunch Whig "without birth and without money" and a close friend of Lord Derby's. He became a great admirer of Elizabeth but early on, he thought she was aloof and somewhat grand and wrote to a friend on August 22nd 1803:-

> ... when the lofty peeress of Derby, showed no inclination to become acquainted with Mrs Creevey tho' she saw her lord talking to me, she came without rhyme or reason to call upon her when we came to town in the winter; and so we have all been there three or four times, and we always found the little man very good and the Countess, Mrs Creevey says, can really behave very well and be very agreeable, but it seems she has a Hell of a temper . . . [1]

Creevey married a widow with money, a Mrs Ord with daughters. He was an untiring letter writer and enjoined one step-daughter, Elizabeth, to keep his letters "for in future times the Creevey Papers may form a curious collection." They do more than that as he was both shrewd and humourous, leaving us lively descriptions of happenings, political and personal, side-lights of gossip and the traits of prominent politicians and persons in high society. In addition to the multitude of letters, (for he kept copies) he kept a detailed diary for thirty-six years which has never come to light. Even so, there is much concerning Knowsley and the Derbys and his accounts are most valuable. He was a good-looking man, full of gossip and small talk and much sought after as a guest: "My Lord and Lady were all kindness to me . . ." [1a] Here is a letter of 1809, the year of the death of the Derby's eldest child, Lucy Elizabeth.

"We dine at Lord Derby's – nobody but us. Lord Derby was excellent in every respect, as he always is, and my Lady still out of spirits for the loss of her child, but surpassing even in her distressed state all your hereditary nobility tho' she came from the stage to her title!"[2]

That very year, Henry Harlow, a pupil of Sir Thomas Lawrence, did a delightful drawing of the three surviving children. How Elizabeth must have treasured it in the light of Lucy's death.

Two years later Creevey gave a further example of Elizabeth's fortitude.

"... we found Lord Derby looking old but very well, and My Lady tho' she was wrapped up with the Mumps, was most gracious as well in her enquiries after you."[3]

The letters talk of many political figures and often of the Prince Regent and the Duke of Cumberland. On Nov. 1st Creevey was at the Pavilion in Brighton.

"We were at the Pavilion last night – Mrs Creevey's three daughters and myself – and had a very pleasant evening ... About half-past nine, which might be a quarter of an hour after we arrived, the Prince came out of the dining-room. He was in his best humour, bowed and spoke to all of us, and looked uncommonly well tho' very fat. He was in full Field Marshal's uniform. He remained quite cheerful and full of fun to the last – half-past twelve – asked after Mrs Creevey's health, and nodded and spoke as he passed us. The Duke of Cumberland was ... looking really hideous, everybody trying to be rude to him – not standing when he came near them. The officers of the Prince's regiment had all dined with him, and looked very ornamental monkeys in their red breeches with gold fringe and yellow boots."[4]

On the next night, November 2nd, 1811 Creevey was again at the Brighton Pavilion where the Prince Regent "sat in the Musick Room (sic) almost all the time . . . and he went on for hours beating his thighs in proper time for the band, and singing out aloud, and looking for accompaniment from Viotti and Lady Jane Houston. It was curious sight to see a Regent thus employed, but he seemed in high good humour..."[5]

Mrs Siddons took her leave of the stage in 1812; she was fifty-seven. Differences between her and Elizabeth have been noted before but the widest came on her retirement. Elizabeth had never been known to pine for the stage but Mrs Siddons wrote, "I feel as if I were mounting the first step of a Ladder conducting me to another world."[6] Although twenty years older than Elizabeth at her retirement, Mrs Siddons unceasingly harked back to her acting days – "for want of excitement". Samuel Rogers recounts that when he visited her one evening she began, "Oh dear – this is the time I used to be thinking of going to the theatre; first came the pleasure of dressing for my part; and then the pleasure of acting it; but all is over now."[7] One would have credited Mrs Siddons with a less shallow character and thought she would have retired with more dignity and grace. Besides, she made the unpardonable mistake of returning to the stage on two occasions. Hazlitt thought this a grave error. "Has she not had enough of glory?" he wrote, "Why should she return to it again? She cannot retire twice with dignity."[8]

Elizabeth was much admired by all at Knowsley as this incident, connected with the Burgoynes, shows.

General Burgoyne, Lord Derby's widower uncle had died in 1792. He bequeathed all he had to his mistress, the singer Susan Caulfield and their four children but there was not even enough to pay his debts. Lord Derby had immediately stepped into the breach, taking the children to The Oaks and making himself responsible for the upbringing and education of the four children, a wonderfully kind act, particularly seeing they were illegitimate. It speaks very highly of Lord Derby's character. The eldest Burgoyne, John, was ten at the time. First he had a private tutor and then he went to Eton and The Royal Academy at Woolwich; he was commissioned into the Royal Engineers. As a boy his holidays were often spent at Derby House and he told how he often accompanied Lord Derby to the theatre, collecting Elizabeth at the stage-door afterwards and taking her and her mother back to Green Street in the carriage. George Wrottesley, John Burgoyne's son-in-law in his life of "Sir John Burgoyne" tells:-

"Lord Derby married Miss Farren who carried with her into her new sphere, graces of mind and person fitted to adorn the highest ranks of society. She proved a steadfast friend to the children of General Burgoyne, and to the last hour of his life, Sir John Burgoyne spoke of her in terms of the warmest affection and respect."[9]

Judging from this letter which Lord Derby wrote to Sir John, then a Lieut. Colonel serving with the Duke of Wellington's Army at Burgos, in Spain, Elizabeth returned his affection.

Knowsley, October 29th 1812.

Dear Burgoyne,

. . . For the telescope, you have no thanks to give me, but to Lady Derby, who is one of your most attached friends, friends, and has shared as warmly as any of us in the joy which your success has occasioned in his family. She desires I will present her best wishes that it may prove useful, and also serve to remind you of an absent and much-attached friend.[10]

John Burgoyne became a Field-Marshal and the dedication of Wrottesley's book to the Fifteenth Earl of Derby proves long-lived gratitude to the Twelfth Earl.

To Edward, 15th Earl of Derby, this record of a brave and honourable life is dedicated, in grateful testimony of the rare kindness and generosity displayed by his ancestor towards the orphan whose career is traced in its pages.[11]

John Burgoyne was only fifteen when Elizabeth married Lord Derby so she was a mother to him in all senses. He was popular with all the Derby family and as this letter from Elizabeth tells him, something of a hero to young James, sixteen at the time.

193

Your letter has afforded Lord Derby and myself (and I may add, all your friends here), the highest satisfaction and amusement; it calls for and has my best thanks, which I beg you to accept with our warmest good wishes for your health and happiness. I cannot well conceive a situation of more interest to a young man than your present one; it combines everything that can make it agreeable, and such an opportunity of observing the military character of all nations will be to you invaluable. To say truth, I do envy you not a little. We have not the consolation here of seeing what we might; is it not too provoking to know Bonaparte so near, and not to get one peep at him? How the Regent could resist the temptation, I cannot guess; he certainly cannot have a grain of curiosity in his whole composition! You will of course have heard he is destined to amuse himself for the remainder of his existence (for I cannot call it life) at St Helena, where he may cultivate his genius for history and poetry in philosophic leisure. However agreeable this sort of retirement may have appeared to various Roman heroes, I hear it by no means suits the inclinations or expectations of the ex-Emperor. He came in full security of remaining here upon the same terms as his brother Lucien Bonaparte had lived among us, and is indignant beyond expression at the disappointment of his hopes. My own opinion is that he will escape and be at large again; he is anxious to get to America or India, and with his plotting head and fascinating manners, he will, I doubt, accomplish his purpose. What are you all going to do in France? New troops arriving every day from all quarters; there must be something intended.

You will not thank me for dwelling upon this subject, when you are wishing to know something of your private friends; and most happy I am to assure you they are all as well as you could wish them to be. M ----- is more busy and occupied with the alterations of her cottage, than the Allies are in settling all the affairs of France; and I question whether the fate of kingdoms has ever cost them so many sleepless nights, as bow windows and blue curtains have caused her. It is quite delightful to see the interest she takes in this little dwelling; which to say truth, she will make very pretty and comfortable, and the employ-ment keeps her in good health and spirits. We had last night the pleasure of reading over some of your old charades, which were much admired, and you much wished for by the whole party. Sir William Hoste is staying here at present, and you would not have been mortified to hear what he said of your character as a soldier and a gentleman. Your ally James, longs to be with you, and begs me to tell you with his best regards, that he hopes you will write often, and long letters. Mary will not forgive me if I do not offer her kindest remembrances; she is so grown since you saw her, that I must not send her love. If there are any ladies in Paris whom I know, that you would like an introduction to, pray let me know, and I will with pleasure send you letters, if you have any time or desire for female society. Lord Derby desires to be affectionately remembered to you again and again.

Your very faithful friend
E. Derby.[12]

Their daughter Mary-Margaret was only fifteen at the time but still Elizabeth considered the proprieties had to be observed. The younger Burgoynes were at Knowsley, the two Derby children, Lord and Lady Stanley and their three children. Loving them as she did, Elizabeth must have been in her element with so many. No wonder Creevey wrote, "I must say I never saw man or woman live more happily with nine grown up children. It is my lord who is the great moving principle . . ."[13]

It must have been at about this time Elizabeth began one of her favourite ploys – giving Lord Derby's favourite grandson, Edward-Geoffrey, lessons in voice-production and elocution. She had noticed his aptitude and she took great pains to lay the foundations well. He was an exceptionally clever young man who afforded the family pride and joy. Sir Archibald Alison wrote, "he was the most perfect orator of his day . . . At once playful and serious, eloquent and instructive, amusing and pathetic; his thoughts seemed to flow from his lips an unpremeditated stream, which at once delights and fascinates his hearers."[14] He was a Tory in politics, Chief Secretary for Ireland, Secretary of State for the Colonies and War and Prime Minister three times, 1852, 1858-59 and 1866-68. He was an M.P. for the last nine years of Elizabeth's life so she must have had a certain satisfaction at the results of her efforts.

The year 1817 must have been a very sad one for Knowsley; James died in April – he was only just seventeen – and Lady Stanley three months later, in June, leaving three sons. The eldest, Edward Geoffrey, was eighteen. He must have felt the loss of James, his seventeen year old half-uncle keenly. The other two boys were fourteen and nine years old. Once more Elizabeth's love of children was sorely needed. One can easily imagine how she took them to her heart, loving, comforting and mothering them.

Their father, Lord Stanley, was very different from his own father. Quiet and studious, he was a noted zoologist and had a large menagerie at Knowsley. He became the patron of Edward Lear, employing him to draw his parrots. Until quite recently, Lear was best known for something quite other than painting and drawing – his celebrated Nonsense Songs and Stories which were composed for the children of Knowsley. The menagerie cost Lord Stanley some £10,000 a year and had a great variety of animals and 318 species of birds comprising some 1,272 individuals.[15] Lear was not short of subjects for his drawing and paintings of animals and birds. It is only comparatively recently that he has become so sought after for his beautiful landscapes which now fetch very high prices. In 1985 a new world record for a work by him, "a superb view of Wady Halfeh in the Sudan", fetched £21,600 at Christies.[16] Lear also made a valuable collection of books on natural history which are still in Knowsley. "You know what a d .... d ramshackle of a library they have here, so I was complaining at breakfast;"[17] Creevey cannot have been complaining of the building or the comprehensive contents so presumably it was in a great muddle.

By the first quarter of the nineteenth century, Liverpool had come a far cry from Queen Elizabeth the First's "poor decay'd town of Liverpool" for coffers were filling fast from the importing of cotton, calico printing and the slave trade. Many landowners were using their increasing affluence to improve their houses.

Lord Derby and Elizabeth kept up the age-old Knowsley tradition of entertaining Royalty and when the Prince Regent came, a special bed of crimson velvet surmounted by the Prince of Wales' feathers in gold, was made for him. Sadly and surprisingly, it has disappeared. By the time of his next visit he was George IV. This was in 1821 and he was given a right royal welcome by using some of the new wealth to build a huge State Dining-Room for the occasion. "It was created by the twelfth Earl, whose taste . . . ran to the classical elegance of the Adam brothers."[18]

It was immense; a banqueting hall, fifty-three feet long by thirty-seven feet wide and "such a height that it destroys the effect of all the other apartments. You enter it from a passage by two Gothic Church-like doors, the whole height of the room . . . Lady Derby . . . when I objected to the immensity of the doors said, 'You've heard General Grosvenor's remark upon them have you not? He asked in his grave, pompous manner – "Pray are those great doors to be opened for every pat of butter that comes into the room?"'[19] Creevey continues, "At the opposite end of the room is an immense Gothic window and the rest of the light is given by a sky-light, mountains high. There are two fire-places and the night we dined there, there were 36 wax candles over the table, 14 on it and 10 great lamps on tall pedestals about the room; and yet those at the bottom of the table said it was quite petrifying in that neighbourhood, and the report here is that they have since been obliged to abandon it entirely from the cold..."[20]

The Hall was fitted up in Gothic style; the doors and furniture of heavily carved oak and the two fireplaces were of elegant, pure white marble. The drapery was rich and appropriate in taste and character and amongst the portraits were those of all the previous Earls and Countesses of Derby. It is greatly to Elizabeth's credit that the grandeur of her surroundings did not go to her head or spoil her in any way. Gilliland echoed Mrs Mathews saying "this noble pair have spent much of the time at their seat in the country where her Ladyship is considered as a blessing to the tenants and the poor."[21] Elizabeth remained the same sweet, kind and gentle person.

During a visit Creevey paid to Knowsley in August 1820, he felt sure there would be no book of State trials in the house; upon which Lady Mary flew from her breakfast and came back in triumph at having found them for me!' Lord Derby would sit in the House of Lords to listen to the debate on the bill to give George IV a divorce from Queen Caroline, Creevey says apropos;

> Upon the subject of the Queen my lord and my lady are both *substantially* right, i.e. in thinking there is not a pin to chuse (sic) between them, and that the Queen has been ill-used, and that nobody but the King could get redress in such a case against his wife. Little Derby goes further than the Countess, when she is not by; but *she* thinks it proper to deprecate all violence, and says that tho' Bennet and I are excellent men, and she likes us both extremely, still, that we are like Dives, and that Lazarus ought to come occasionally and cool our tongues. Is that not the image of her? (St Luke. XVI.19–31).[22]

It is evident that Elizabeth liked Creevey from this letter, written from Knowsley:

> We are all mighty gracious here. My Lady [Derby] told me before we went into dinner yesterday to sit with my best ear next to her . . . We sat down 22 to dinner, all of them Hornbys, except 4 Hortons, 2 Ramthornes, young Ashton and myself. My lord was in excellent spirits, and, for *such* company, it went off all very well . . . I never saw Lady Stanley looking so well, or in such good spirits... I won a shilling last night, I'd have you know, and then ate some shrimps, and Lady Derby would have some negus[23] made for me alone; and all the toadys laughed very much because my lady did, so it was all very well...[24]

"I like Lady Mary better every time I see her" [25] wrote Creevey in 1820. The Derbys' only surviving child was a pretty dark-haired edition of her mother though not so tall, and she inherited many of Elizabeth's attributes. She was musical and had a sweet singing voice and played the harp. She too was an expert needlewoman and – unlike her mother – an excellent horsewoman. "Lady Mary who afterwards became Lady Wilton, was at this time a poet's ideal of all that is most lovely and most attractive in girlhood."[26] So wrote Lady Frances Shelley when Lady Mary was nineteen. In view of her approaching marriage this announcement in The Gentleman's Magazine is interesting.

> Gazette. Whitehall, November 17th 1821. Earl of Wilton and Viscount Grey de Wilton, 2nd son of the Earl of Grosvenor, by Eleanour his wife, only surviving child of Thomas, Earl of Wilton, deceased, to take and use the surname of Egerton only, and also bear the Arms of Egerton only.[27]

On November 29th, they were married.

"On Thursday last, the Right Hon. Earl of Wilton, second son of Earl Grosvenor, to Lady Mary Stanley, daughter of the Right Hon. the Earl of Derby, Lord Lieutenant of Lancashire. The ceremony was performed by the Rev. John Hornby, Rector of Winwick (in consequence of the unavoidable absence of the Archbishop of York who was expected), at the Parish Church of Huyton at half-past eleven o'clock, in the presence of the noble families of the illustrious houses of Derby and Grosvenor; at two o'clock the happy pair set out for Heaton House, near Manchester, the seat of the Right Hon. the Earl of Wilton – The bells of Huyton, of Prescot, and all the adjoining churches rung joyful peals during the day, and at noon, the great bells of Chester Cathedral, followed by those of other churches, announced the happy event in that city. The Earl of Wilton is in his twenty-second year his Countess in her twenty-first."[28]

Kaleidescope, a magazine published on Christmas Day that year, gave this description of Lady Mary's wedding-dress.

The bridal dress worn by Lady Mary Stanley now Countess of Wilton, on her marriage, consisted of elegant Brussels lace, trimmed with costly lace of the same description, over rich white satin, with a large Brussels veil to correspond.

One of the wedding-presents was the famous full length portrait of Elizabeth by Sir Thomas Lawrence. Eventually it was bought by the American banker and famous collector, Mr Pierpont Morgan. Here are two stories about it.

The first came from Mr Morgan's granddaughter three years ago (1985). When she was a little girl she often had supper with her grandfather on Sunday nights and she told me that when the gong sounded, he would take her by the hand and they would walk to the dining-room, he would open the door and bow saying "Good evening, Miss Farren".

The second concerns King Edward VII who, when dining with Pierpont Morgan expressed the view that such a portrait was too beautiful for the dining-room to which his host replied, "I like it there."

The Wilton family sold the picture at the end of the last century to a purchaser called Neumann. Presumably it was from him Pierpont Morgan bought it. In 1935 it was sold to Edward Harkness, reputedly for £40,000. He bequeathed it to his wife for life and then to the Metropolitan Museum of Art, New York. Had it not left this country, had the Gilbert Stuart of Elizabeth not gone to America and the Zoffany to Australia, there is little doubt Elizabeth would not be the forgotten figure she is today.

Lord Derby and his son-in-law had much in common; Lord Wilton was renowned in the chase and on the turf but only three years after his marriage, Creevey was writing on October 24th 1824:-

> I think this Lord Wilton has the worst countenance I think,
> I ever saw, and he appears a sulky, selfish chap; but she
> seems very happy . . . and there is great charm in all she
> does.
> October 20th 1824.[29]

The Derbys' time was divided between Derby House, the Oaks and Knowsley. So many of Creevey's letters are written from Knowsley or about it, the impression could be that the Derbys' entertainment of guests was always there; this was not so. Although not quite such large parties were given at The Oaks, they had house parties there also.

The Oaks, near the village of Woodmanstone was a large castellated building partly covered in ivy which took its name from a grove of oak trees called Lambert's Oaks after the name of the family which owned it from the 13th century until 1788. Then it was sold to the eleventh Earl of Derby by William Lambert. When Lord Derby inherited the Oaks from his grandfather he increased the size of the estate by fencing in much of the common and made a plantation about two miles in circumference. There were gardens, conservatories, peach houses and many fine trees.

The men at the Oaks house parties hunted carted stags, once having a run "beyond Tunbridge Wells and returned at ½ past 8 in the evening, in a post chaise" After dinner they all played "at Blind Man's Buffe"{sic} etc. While the men hunted, the ladies went for "delightful" drives in the Phaeton with Elizabeth. The house party attended Woodmanstone Church on Sundays but beforehand, both Lord Derby and Elizabeth read prayers.

Prayers were also de rigeur at Knowsley and Creevey tells this story in a letter to his step-daughter on November 23rd 1824.

. . . in the evening Lord Derby read prayers from the furthest end of the Library, the doors being open; that room was filled with company, the Hall was filled with servants kneeling round the Billiard Table, some six or eight of us behind them in the Drawing Room, the doors of which were likewise open. After the ceremony my Lady joined me again in the Gallery, and I was remarking how well Lord Derby read, and how distinctly I heard every word he said at that distance. 'Yes' said she, 'he likes it extremely and is a great stickler for doing the thing himself. When the Archbishop of York was here the other day, he wanted to read the prayers, but Ld Derby would not hear of it, he w'd not even let him say Grace, but always contrived to get the start of him, so that the Archbishop at last said, "Come let us settle this matter, we are Brother Directors of Ancient Music, so let us sing a Grace together as a Duet . . ." '31

Twenty-eight and twenty-nine years, respectively, after Elizabeth's retirement from the stage she was far from being forgotten for James Boaden wrote "The Life of J.P. Kemble", 1827, in two volumes. In this he discusses the leading actresses of 1783, the year after Elizabeth became Queen of Comedy at Drury Lane.

I shall first pay my respects to Miss Farren, who in Comedy, if not in Tragedy, merited the highest distinction. She had succeeded at Drury Lane Theatre to the characters which had been performed by Mrs Abington; though it would be difficult to mention two actresses who differed essentially in their comic style. They both delighted to exhibit the woman of fashion; but the character received the differences of its colouring from the personal qualities of the representatives.

Miss Farren, at this time, in her person was tall and perfectly graceful; her face beautiful and expressive; her voice was rather thin, and of but slender power, but rendered effective by an articulation of the greatest neatness and precision. It was her practice from the weakness of her organ, to stand rather forward upon the stage.

When I carry my recollection back to the peculiar character of her acting, I think I may say that it was distinguished by the grace of *delicacy* beyond that of every comic actress I have ever seen. It was as it were the *soul* of all she did; and even in the comedies of Congreve she never lost it for a moment, amid free allusions and sometimes licentious expressions of dialogue. The eyes sparkled with intelligence, but it was a chaste and purified beam, from a mind unsullied though sportive. Her levity therefore was never wanton; her mirth had no approach to rudeness. She played the coxcomb of either sex with the highest zest, but refinement was the invariable attendant upon her ridicule, and taste seemed to preside alike over her action and her utterance.

From her early habit of acting tragedy, she had drawn enough to give to the occasional pathos of comedy a charm of infinite value. The reproach of Julia, in The Rivals to Falkland, was extremely affecting; and few scenes drew more tears than her sensibility commanded in the return of Lady Townley, to the use of her heart and her understanding. Many years have now elapsed since I first beheld this distinguished lady, but I can safely say, that, in her own line, she has never been equalled or approached.'[32]

Writing in his Memoirs of Mrs Siddons the following year Boaden said:-

. . . Tragedy, the other Muse was about to suffer a loss which thirty years have scarcely shown a tendency to replace. I mean the elevation of Miss Farren to a coronet in the year 1797. Perhaps I do not refer effects to causes inadequate to their production when I say that this theatrical demise absolutely produced the degeneracy of comedy into farce. The lady of our Congreves lost that court-like refinement in manners, that polished propriety in speech; the coarser parts in comedy were forced forwards without balance, without contracts; cultivated life on the stage became insipid as soon as its representative was without the necessary charms. This produced the absolute fall of genteel comedy, which had long been in a state of decline, and broad laughter reigned in the unbounded hilarity of Mrs Jordan.[33]

205

What a curious sensation Elizabeth must have had, reading such glowing accounts from Boaden, the soul of accuracy and integrity, and how proud the feelings of Lord Derby and the "extended" family.

Sir William Hotham, nephew of Elizabeth's old friend, Sir Charles Hotham wrote, "I met her frequently at the house of my uncle, Sir Chas. Hotham who was a very great friend of hers . . . Her countenance was in the highest degree animating, and her figure elegant."

"Slender of form, dainty of dress with a distinction of manner and refinement of bearing, Miss Farren's merry blue eyes, her winning smile and her expressive face captivated an audience already impressed by her mock airs and graces, her flirting fan, her 'tripping tongue' and all the assumed insolence of the haughty beauty whom she loved to impersonate." Sir William affirmed that she filled the exalted position to which she was called in a manner creditable to her good feelings and strong understanding and was deservedly beloved. He also underlined her charitable nature and her exemplary conduct as a wife and mother – to which he might have added step-mother, grandmother, step-grandmother and substitute-mother to the four young Burgoynes! Sir William further related that he "dined at Knowsley in the last summer she was alive, and though in her usual high flow of spirits and intent upon the kindest duties of hospitality, she was evidently sinking into her grave."[34]

The same year, 1828 on December, 6th Creevey wrote from Croxteth;

> "Have you ever heard that Lady Derby is pronounced to have an incurable disease, an ossification or some other fatal affliction of the heart . . . I went there to call yesterday and as I walked up towards the house, perceiving Lord Derby peeping at me thro' a distant window to make out who I was, I purposely loitered and turned about in all directions, in order that he might recognise me, and so I was admitted in an instant, and he

206

met me in the hall, and having asked of course directly after Lady Derby, he said, 'She is a little better today *and will see you.*' I sat, however a long time with him and Mr Phipps Hornby before I saw her and when I did so, it was for a very short time before she got into her carriage; but during that short time she played her part brilliantly. I said 'I'm glad to hear you are better today.' 'Thank you,' she said, and nodded her head at me in a way that none could misunderstand for 'I'm going to die,' she then put out her hand a second time and said, 'Will you come and see us?' to which of course I said, 'With great pleasure,' and when little Derby said 'When will you come, Creevey?' I said 'next week'; and I mean to go . . .'[35]

He did go, eight days later on December 13th, but he did not see Elizabeth and he said, 'Knowsley without Lady Derby is like a house with all the fires and candles put out.'

How sad it is to have to record that the last years of the beautiful Elizabeth Farren were years of pain and suffering – was this why she became addicted to snuff?[36] Did it ease her pain? But she did bear the time uncomplaining, with characteristic fortitude.

She died at Knowsley on April 23rd 1829. She with the merry blue eyes and the winning ways who had thrilled the hearts of audiences in over a hundred parts; she who had taken sunshine into the homes of the poor, the sick and the bereaved and she who had been "loved and respected by the distinguished circle who gladly received her as an ornament", breathed no more.

Having been in the public eye since the age of ten, first on the stage and then as the Countess of Derby, it is no surprise that the funeral of one so deeply loved and so deeply mourned, was a very grand affair indeed. The following account illustrates the magnificence of the occasion.

Thursday being appointed for the Interment of the remains of the estimable Countess of Derby in the family vault at

Ormskirk, the utmost excitement was visible at an early hour in the neighbourhood. Crowds of persons assembled in different parts of the road through which the procession would have to pass, and, towards noon, the very house-tops in the town of Ormskirk were tenanted by parties anxious to behold the interesting ceremony.

At about 8 o'clock, the mournful cavalcade left the mansion at Knowsley, shortly after 12 o'clock, it arrived at Ormskirk in the following order.

Two mutes on beautiful black, long-tailed horses, covered with black cloth and hoods. The riders in complete suits of mourning with cloakes, carrying staves tastefully ornamented with crape.

The tenantry of the township of Knowsley, 42 in number, on horse-back, habited in cloakes and wearing hat bands.

The land steward and principal servants of the establishment on horse-back, two and two.

Large and magnificent plume of costly ostrich feathers borne on foot.

The 1st mourning coach drawn by 4 horses and containing the clergy and medical gentlemen.

The 2nd mourning coach, drawn by 4 horses and containing the supporters of the pall on the left, namely -

Hon. E.G.Stanley, Rev. J.T. Hornby, Capt. Hornby R.N., R.A. Hornby Esq.

The 3rd mourning coach, the pall on the right, namely -

E.A. Hornby Esq., Rev. A. Hornby, E.G. Hornby Esq., Hon. C.J.F. Stanley.

Two mutes on horseback as at the first.

The coronet of the late Countess, on a crimson velvet cushion, borne by a gentleman.

The hearse drawn by six horses with carriers and pages

each side.

Two mutes as before.

A mourning coach drawn by six horses and containing the chief mourners, Lords Stanley and Wilton (Elizabeth's stepson and son-in-law).

The carriage of the Earl of Derby, drawn by six horses.

A number of other carriages followed which belonged to relatives, and then,

A very long train of private carriages followed and the procession arriving at the church gate, the coffin was removed from the hearse and carried into the body of the church were strictly private, the public being excluded . . .

The coffin which was an exceedingly handsome one, was covered with crimson Genoa velvet, ornamented with silver and a silver plate on the lid announced the age and title of the deceased.

Looking back to the list of pall-bearers of the left, it is headed by that favourite of Lord Derby's grandchildren, Edward-Geoffrey who has already been mentioned and who was Elizabeth's elocution pupil; his youngest brother, Charles James Fox Stanley, Grenadier Guards was a pall-bearer on the right.

The Augustinian Priory at Burscough near Ormskirk had been founded in the twelfth century but dissolved at the time of the dissolution of the monasteries and the bells taken to the Church of St Peter and St Paul in Ormskirk in 1540, as well as the 15th century alabaster effigies of the 1st Earl of Derby and his wife. Ormskirk was some thirteen miles from Knowsley and the journey took three and a half hours for the funeral procession to reach the church. The local paper reported, "up to Wednesday night it was the fixed intention of the Venerable Earl himself to be present, but at the solicitation of his children we understand his lordship consented to remain at home. We are happy to find that his lordship's health is quite as good as under the circumstances could be expected."

Poor Lord Derby. He had loved Elizabeth for over half a century, had waited so long and so patiently to marry her . . . she had given him the happiest years of his life in their thirty-two years of marriage and now she had gone. He was alone but at least he had their lovely daughter nearby. "Lady Derby is dead – but her virtues yet live in her daughter the Countess of Wilton," wrote Mrs Mathews.

On hearing how grief-stricken the old Earl was, Emily Eden remarked:

> "I think it ought to be made a rule of the odd game we all play here that these old attached couples should die together, Baucis and Philemon fashion, for the survivor's is a hard place."[37]

Of the many long, complimentary obituaries these extracts give an example of the tone, "Her private life was irreproachable; her devoted attachment to her mother . . . was the best eulogy on the qualities of her heart." References were made to "the esteem in which she was held by George III and Queen Charlotte as well as by George IV." The Memoir in the Gentleman's Magazine concluded, "many females have risen to exalted rank but unfortunately too few by a union of superior beauty with virtuous conduct. To the subject of this memoir this praise is due."

Not only at home but also abroad, Elizabeth's name and fame had spread; obituaries were in the publications of France, Italy and Spain and this short extract from Larousse, illustrates foreign opinion.

> ". . . son succès fût complet. Sa grâce, sa sensibilité, le charme de sa voix, sa grand beauté et la décence de sa conduite lui valurent les hommage des hommes les plus illustres de L'Angleterre. Au nombre de ses adorateurs se trouvait le Comte de Derby qui conçut pour elle la grande passion . . ."

Everybody missed Elizabeth and Creevey expressed his feelings in verse.

> But *she* still shines tho' out of sight
> For she has carried off the light
> And left us dark in blackest night.

> And never more shall Countess reign
> O'er Knowsley and its Stanley train
> So bright as this from Drury Lane.

Lord Derby died five years later, on October 21lst 1839. He was laid, by his own request, beside his beloved Elizabeth. While at Knowsley, the family had attended services at Huyton Parish Church and Elizabeth's memorial is there.

> "Near the place where she loved to worship and where her voice was often lifted up in prayer and praise, this tribute of grateful affection is dedicated to the virtuous memory of Elizabeth Farren, Countess of Derby, wife of Edward, twelfth Earl of Derby.
> From her earliest years, and through every change of her most eventful life, she made Religion her companion and guide, while native graces of mind and manners made her seem born for that station to which she was subsequently raised. She visited the fatherless and widows in their affliction. She kept herself unspotted from the world and she died as she had lived, in the fear of God, and in humble hope of his redeeming mercy."

> Thou has a few names even in Sardis which have not defiled their garments; and they shall walk with me in white for they are worthy.

> Revelations iii, 4.

Chapter Twelve - Footnotes

1. Creevey's Life and Times Ed. John Gore 1933 Aug 22 1803 p.20.
1a. Maxwell. Sir Herbert. The Creevey Papers 1903. Nov. ll, 1809 p.ll2.
2. Maxwell op.cit. p.112
3. Gore. op. cit. Elizabeth was 52 when she had mumps, in 1811.
4. Maxwell. op. cit. p.148.
5. Ibid p.148.
6. Rogers, Samuel. Reminiscences & Table Talk. ed.Powett, G.H. 1903
7. Rogers etc. op.cit.
8. Hazlitt. Wm. op.cit.
9. Wrottesley. G. Life & Correspondence of Field Marshal Sir John Burgoyne 2 vols. 1873. vol.i. p.247.
10. Pg 8. Preface to above.
11. Dedication to above.
12. Wrottesley. op. cit. vol.i. p.314.
13. Maxwell op.cit. p.399
14. Knowsley Hall guide book p.18.
15. Ibid p.16.
16. Christie's Recent Sales. 19 Nov.1985. (Now known as Wadi Halfa).
17. Maxwell op.cit. p.399
18. Knowsley Guide Book p.30
19. Maxwell op.cit. p.399.
20. Ibid
21. Gilliland op.cit. 725
22. Maxwell op.cit. p.305
23. Ibid p.172. Negus. A drink made with port and sherry wine mixed with hot water, sugar, nutmeg and lemon juice; so called after Colonel Negus, the inventor. Blackie's Modern Cyclopaedia.1891. Vol. VI. p.98
24. Ibid

25. Shelley. Diary of Lady Frances, 1912. 2 Vols. vol.i. p.12.

26. Gentlemen's Magazine. July-Dec. 1821 vol.91. p. 641.

27. Gore's General Advertiser. Thursday December 6th 1821.

28. Maxwell op. cit. p.424

29. Huxley, Gervas. Lady Elizabeth and The Grosvenors 1965. p.68

30. Gore. J. op.cit. p.204.

31. Braden, Kemble. vol.i. pp. 81–82.

32. Braden, Siddons. pp.418, 419.

33. Hotham, M.S.S.

34. Gore. op.cit. p.303.

35. Lady Derby reputed to be one of the best customers of Fribourg and Treyer in the Haymarket.

36. Huxley. op.cit. 43. See Lamprière's classical Dictionary 1788 p.115.

37. Gore. op.cit. p.303.

Epilogue

Looking back on the contrasting lives of the Queen of Tragedy – Mrs Siddons – and the Queen of Comedy – Elizabeth – it is interesting to reflect on the shape of their lives which was as much in contrast as the muse each represented on the stage.

Elizabeth – merry, vivacious, amusing, witty and excellent company. She had led a gay social life retiring from the stage to marry her noble admirer.

Mrs Siddons – unhappily married, starved of affection, stiff and formal which militated against her social popularity. She lost two daughters in sad circumstances and, retiring for age, she felt life was virtually over.

Elizabeth was loved for her kindness, generosity and compassion, admired for her elegance and her bewitching looks and celebrated for ease, grace and delicacy, natural gifts which were polished by correct taste and regulated by good sense and discernment.

The high tone of Lord Derby's regard for her was expressed by him in this verse:

> "While wond'ring angels, as they look'd from high,
> Observ'd thy absence with a holy sigh;
> To them a bright, ethereal seraph said –
> Blame not the conduct of th' exalted maid;
> Whe'er she goes, her steps can never stray;
> Religion walks, companion of her way;
> She goes with ev'ry virtuous thought impress'd;
> Heaven on her face and heaven within her breast."[1]

1. Gilliland. Th. The Dramatic Mirror. 1808. vol.II p. 725.

Appendix

The marriage of the Earl of Wilton and Lady Mary Margaret Stanley, brought theatical and musical heritage to a number of aristocratic families. Two of their five children are mentioned below.

First, Lord Derby and Elizabeth's granddaughter and namesake Lady Elizabeth Grey-Egerton, married Lord de Ros, grandson of Lord Henry FitzGerald who had made such a success of acting Don Felix under Elizabeth Farren's direction at Richmond House.

Second, her next sister Lady Katherine Grey-Egerton, married the Hon. Henry Coke, brother to the Earl of Leicester. This union has great relevance today.

The Cokes lived in London. Lady Katherine was an accomplished pianist and their milieu of artists and aristocracy was much the same in which her Derby grandparents had moved. Friend and Lady-in-Waiting to the Duchess of Teck, Lady Katherine later became Woman-of-the-Bedchamber to her daughter, Princess "May", then Duchess of York but in time to become Queen Mary, Consort of King George V.

A gap of nearly 160 years since Elizabeth's death can be bridged by the vivid memories of Lady Katherine's granddaughter, Stella Coke, now Mrs Ryan, who paints this word picture of her grandmother whom she remembers "as if it were yesterday". "To her grandchildren she was a fount of wisdom, infinitely kind and infinitely gentle. She also possessed great firmness and ran her household with complete command – rather like Queen Victoria." Lady Katherine used to play with her grandchildren and gave them their first lessons in reading and telling the time.

The Coke's daughter Sybil, married Captain Charles Crutchley, Scots Guards; Lady Crutchley as she became, was an excellent

217

amateur actress, acting with The Old Stagers during Canterbury Cricket week into the late 1920's. Humphrey Tilling, President of The Old Stagers also says, "She spoke the Old Stagers Lines at the end of our Epilogue on the Friday night nearly every year up until 1938. She was of course the most delightful and wonderful person."

Mr Tilling says of Lady Crutchley's son, "Gerald was the last Old Stager who played County Cricket in the St Lawrence Ground during Cricket Week – and played in the theatre with O.S. in the evenings."

We reach Elizabeth Farren's great-great-great granddaughter with the excellent and much admired actress, Rosalie Crutchley. There are two coincidental parallels with Elizabeth's early career in that both actresses made their débuts in Liverpool and their first London curtseys at The Haymarket Theatre.

Appendix I.i
SOME PARTS, PLACES AND APPROXIMATE DATES BEFORE ELIZABETH FARREN'S LONDON DEBUT

DATE	PART	PLAY	PLACE	MANAGER
1769. Dec.	Columbine	Pantomime	Salisbury	Her father
1773	Edward V	Richard III	Wakefield & others	Whitley
1774	Rosetta	Love in a Village	Liverpool	Younger
1774	Lady Townley	The Provoked Husband	Liverpool & others	Younger
1775	Dorinda	The Tempest	Manchester	Younger
1776	Miss Prue	Love for Love	Liverpool	Younger
1777 Feb.	Fatima	Cymon	Manchester	Younger
1777 Feb.	Jessica	The Merchant of Venice	Manchester	Younger
1777	Miss Marchmont	False Delicacy	Manchester	Younger
1777	Ophelia	Hamlet	Manchester	Younger
1778 (after her London début)	Cordelia	King Lear	Manchester	Younger

Places other than Liverpool etc. included Chester, Shrewsbury and Birmingham.

During her career in London Elizabeth Farren acted in *Jehu* at Drury Lane on 19th February 1779. No parts are assigned except that of Lord Jehu which is said to have been taken by Thomas King.

Elizabeth Farren was portrayed by Ramberg as Hermia in *A Midsummer Night's Dream*, also by two unknown artists as the Queen in *Richard II* and Creusa but no dates or details have been found.

PARTS PLAYED BY ELIZABETH FARREN DURING HER LONDON CAREER (WITH FIRST NIGHTS) OF SAME (in London).

DATE	PART	PLAY	PLAYWRIGHT	THEATRE
1777				
9th June	Kate Hardcastle	She Stoops to Conquer	Oliver Goldsmith	Haymarket
30th June	Maria	The Citizen	Arthur Murphy	Haymarket
12th Aug	Rosetta	Love in a Village	Isaac Bickerstaffe	Haymarket
18th Aug	Miss Tittup	Bon Ton	David Garrick	Haymarket
30th Aug	Rosina	The Spanish Barber	adapted by Geo. Colman from Beaumarchais.	Haymarket
1778				
11th July	Nancy Lovel	The Suicide	Geo. Colman	Haymarket
21st Aug	Lady Townley	The Provok'd Husband	Sir J. Vanburgh (alt.Cibber)	Haymarket
2nd Sept	Lady Fanciful	The Provok'd Wife	Sir J. Vanburgh	Haymarket
23rd Sept	Clarinda	The Suspicious Husband	B. Hoadly 1st time at Covent Garden	
8th Oct	Charlotte Rusport	The West Indian	Rich. Cumberland 1st time Drury Lane	
15th Oct	Lady Sash	The Camp	R.B. Sheridan	Drury Lane
22nd Oct	Evelina	Caractacus	W. Mason	Drury Lane

Date	Play	Author	Role	Theatre
31st Oct	The Chances	J. Fletcher	2nd Constantia	Drury Lane
21st Dec	A Trip to Scarborough	R.B. Sheridan	Berinthia	Drury Lane

1779

Date	Play	Author	Role	Theatre
3rd Feb	The Discovery	Frances Sheridan	Mrs Knightly	Drury Lane
13th Mar	The Gamesters	J. Shirley	Penelope	Drury Lane
9th Apr	The Devil to Pay	C. Coffey	Nell	Drury Lane
21st Apr	The Law of Lombardy	R. Jephson	Alinda	Drury Lane
28th Apr	The Double Deception	Eliz. Richardson	Louisa Freemore	Drury Lane
1st May	The Way of the World	Wm Congreve	Millamant	Drury Lane
21st May	A Bold Stroke for a Wife	Sussanah Centlivre	Ann Lovely	Drury Lane
17th Aug	The Stratagem	G. Farquhar	Mrs Sullen	Haymarket
31st Aug	The Separate Maintenance	Geo. Colman	Lady Newbery	Haymarket
12th Oct	Love for Love	Wm Congreve	Angelica	Drury Lane
16th Oct	Othello	Shakespeare	Desdemona	Drury Lane
30th Oct	The Critic	R.B. Sheridan	An Italian Girl	Drury Lane
17th Nov	The Runaway	Hannah Cowley	Bella	Drury Lane
29th Nov	The Winter's Tale	Shakespeare	Hermione	Drury Lane

1780

Date	Play	Author	Role	Theatre
22nd Feb	The Rivals	R.B. Sheridan	Lydia Languish	Drury Lane
4th Mar	The Old Batchelor	Wm Congreve	Belinda	Drury Lane
3rd Apr	The Inconstant	G. Farquhar	Bisarre	Drury Lane
20th May	Twelfth Night	Shakespeare	Olivia	Drury Lane

Date	Play	Role	Author	Theatre
24th May	The Miniature Picture	Miss Loveless	Eliz. Craven	Drury Lane
5th Aug	The Chapter of Accidents	Cecilia	Sophia Lee	Haymarket
24th Aug	The Merchant of Venice	Portia	Shakespeare	Haymarket
5th Sept	Henry and Emma	Emma	Henry Bate	Haymarket
22nd Nov	The Generous Imposter	Dorinda	T.L. O'Beirne	Drury Lane
27th Dec	The Lord of the Manor	Sophia	J. Burgoyne	Drury Lane

1781

Date	Play	Role	Author	Theatre
26th Jan	The Hypocrite	Lady Lambert	I. Bickerstaffe	Drury Lane
17th Feb	The Royal Suppliants	Macaria	J. Delap	Drury Lane
3rd Apr	The Rivals	Julia	R.B. Sheridan	Drury Lane
17th Apr	Alexander the Great	Statira	N. Lee	Drury Lane
24th Apr	The Way to Keep Him	Mrs Lovemore	Arthur Murphy	Drury Lane
1st May	Romeo and Juliet	Juliet	Shakespeare	Drury Lane
9th May	The Wonder	Donna Violante	Susannah Centlivre	Drury Lane
12th May	The Careless Husband	Lady Betty Modish	Colley Cibber	Drury Lane
17th May	Oronooko	Imoinda	T. Southerne	Drury Lane
18th July	The English Merchant	Amelia	Geo. Colman	Haymarket
21st Aug	The Confederacy	Clarissa	Sir J. Vanburgh	Haymarket
24th Aug	The Merry Wives of Windsor	Mrs Ford	Shakespeare	Haymarket
19th Oct	King Arthur	Emmeline	J. Dryden	Drury Lane
10th Nov	The Divorce	Lady Harriet Trifle	I. Jackman	Drury Lane
12th Nov	The Double Gallant	Lady Sadlife	Colley Cibber	Drury Lane

Date	Role	Play	Author	Theatre
27th Nov	Almeida	The Fair Circassian	Sam. Jackson Pratt	Drury Lane
1782				
25th Feb	Miss Harriet Temple	Variety	R. Griffiths	Drury Lane
21st Mar	Rosetta	The Foundling	E. Moore	Drury Lane
15th Apr	Miss Griskin	Dissipation	M.P. Andrews	Drury Lane
8th May	Indiana	The Conscious Lovers	Sir R. Steele	Drury Lane
26th Sept	Lady Teazle	The School for Scandal	R.B. Sheridan	Drury Lane
14th Oct	Mrs Harley	False Delicacy	H. Kelly	Drury Lane
29th Oct	The Widow Belmore	The Way to Keep Him	Arthur Murphy	Drury Lane
1783				
24th Jan	Miranda	The Busy Body	Mrs Centlivre	Drury Lane
29th Jan	Ophelia Wyndham	The School for Vanity	S.J. Pratt	Drury Lane
20th Mar	Lady Rentless	Dissipation	M.P. Andrews	Drury Lane
28th Apr	Biddy Tipkin	The Tender Husband	Sir R. Steele	Drury Lane
29th Apr	Mary	The City Madam	P. Massiger	Drury Lane
12th May	Maria	Imitation	F.G. Waldron	Drury Lane
27th Nov	Estifania	Rule a Wife & Have a Wife	J. Fletcher	Drury Lane
1784				
14th Feb	Louisa	The Reparation	M.P. Andrews	Drury Lane
19th Apr	Leonora	Love in a Veil	R. Savage	Drury Lane

Date	Play	Character	Author	Venue
5th May	The Jealous Wife	Mrs Oakly	Geo. Colman	Drury Lane
17th May	Amphitryon	Alcmena	J. Dryden	Drury Lane
2nd June	Election of the Managers	Mrs Simper	Geo. Colman	Drury Lane
2nd Sept	The Two Connoisseurs	Lady Harriet	W. Hayley	Drury Lane
28th Oct	Deception	Clarissa	Unknown	Drury Lane
3rd Dec	The Double Dealer	Lady Plyant	Wm Congreve	Druy Lane
22nd Dec	The Natural Son	Lady Paragon	Rich. Cumberland	Drury Lane

1785

Date	Play	Character	Author	Venue
11th Apr	Beau's Duel	Lady Plotwell	Wm. Congreve	Drury Lane
26th Apr	The Widow Bewitch'd	Young Lady Languish	J. Mottley	Drury Lane
26th July	All's Well That Ends Well	Helena	Shakespeare	Haymarket
4th Aug	I'll Tell You What	Mrs Chas. Euston	Mrs Inchbald	Haymarket
26th Oct	All in the Wrong	Belinda	Arthur Murphy	Drury Lane
2nd Dec	The Jubilee	The Comic Muse	David Garrick	Drury Lane

1786

Date	Play	Character	Author	Venue
14th Jan	The Heiress	Lady Emily Gayville*	J. Burgoyne	Drury Lane
17th May	The Provok'd Wife	Lady Brute	Sir J. Vanburgh	Drury Lane
24th July	The Disbanded Officer	Baroness of Bruchsal	James Johnstone	Drury Lane
29th Aug	Tit for Tat	Florinda	Geo. Colman	Drury Lane
12th Dec	A School for Greybeards	Donna Seraphina	Hannah Cowley	Drury Lane

* Previously at Richmond House

1787				
12th Mar	Lady Morden	Seduction	Th. Holcroft	Drury Lane
7th July	Lady Rustic	The Country Attorney	Rich. Cumberland	Drury Lane
17th Aug	Beatrice	Much Ado About Nothing	Shakespeare	Drury Lane
21st Aug	Susan	The Follies of a Day	Th. Holcroft	Drury Lane
10th Nov	Lady Charlotte Courtley	The New Peerage	Harriet Lee	Drury Lane

1788				
21st Apr	Rosina	Transformation	C. Bonner	Drury Lane
28th Apr	Mrs Bellville	The School for Wives	H. Kelly	Drury Lane
7th May	Florinda	Seeing is Believing	R.P. Jodrell	Drury Lane
19th June	Caroline	The Disbanded Officer	James Johnstone	Haymarket
9th Aug	Miss Eliza Morton	The Sword of Peace	M. Starke	Haymarket

1789				
20th Apr	Countess	False Appearances dedicated to E.F. First at Richmond House.	General Conway	Drury Lane
10th Oct	Lady Bell	Know Your Own Mind	Arthur Murphy	Drury Lane
13th Oct	Dorinda	The Tempest	Shakespeare	Drury Lane
24th Oct	Leonora	The False Friend	Sir J. Vanburgh	Drury Lane
2nd Dec	Charlotte	The Hypocrite	I. Bickerstaffe	Drury Lane

Date	Character	Author	Play	Theatre
1792				
20th Apr	Miss Herbert	Jos. Richardson	The Fugitive	Drury Lane
20th Oct	Niece	Sir R. Steele	The Tender Husband	Drury Lane
1793				
3rd April	Constance Evelyn	E. Mason	False Colours	Drury Lane
1794				
8th May	Louisa Ratcliffe	R. Cumberland	The Jew	Drury Lane
1795				
28th Feb	Emily Tempest	R. Cumberland	The Wheel of Fortune	Drury Lane
17th Apr	Lady Bellair	Ed. Jenningham	The Welch Heiress	Drury Lane
12th May	Lady Ruby	R. Cumberland	First Love	Drury Lane
20th Oct	Jane	R. Cumberland	The Dependant	Drury Lane
1796				
23rd Jan	Olivia	Th. Holcroft	One Man of Ten Thousand	Drury Lane
12th Mar	Helen	Geo. Colman the Younger	The Iron Chest	Drury Lane
23rd May	Melantha	J.P. Kemble	Celadon and Florimel	Drury Lane
6th Dec	Lady Dorville	Th. Holcroft	The Force of Ridicule	Drury Lane

Alphabetical Index of Plays mentioned in the text

Acknowledgements

This biography would never have been written but for the great encouragement, enthusiasm and help of my late husband, Guy Bloxam. To my son Nicholas, I owe a deep debt of gratitude for his invaluable assistance in countless ways. Gratitude is also due to Sir Michael Levey for so kindly writing the Foreword on the famous full-length Sir Thomas Lawrence portrait, and to the present Earl of Derby for his kind permission to reproduce the Gainsborough portrait of the Twelfth Earl, and the Harlow drawing of the Twelfth Earl's three children by his second wife, née Elizabeth Farren.

I must also thank two of Elizabeth Farren's descendants, Stella Ryan, née Coke, and Rosalie Crutchley, for their encouragement and help.

I cannot hope to name the very many people who have assisted me, but special mention should be made of the following:

Mr Anthony Berry
Miss Margaret Brentnall
Dr Emma Devapriam, Senior Curator of European Art, National Gallery of Victoria,
     Melbourne, Australia
Dr Kenneth Garlick
Dr and Mrs W.O. Hassall
Mr Nigel Higson, late Hull University Archivist
Dr F.R. Innes, Boston, Mass, USA
Mr James Morwood, Vaughan Librarian, Harrow School
Miss Constance Anne Parker, late Librarian, Royal Academy of Arts
Miss Sybil Rosenfeld, Society of Theatre Research
Dr Alexander Schouvaloff, the Curator and also the staff of the Theatre Museum,
     the Victoria and Albert Museum
Mrs Stewart-Smith, née Elizabeth Farren (no connection) for sharing her research on
     Miss Farren
Mr Humphrey Tilling, President of The Old Stagers
Mrs Hugh Welby-Everard
The staffs of The British Library, Reference Division, the Manuscript Room and the
     Prints & Drawings Room, British Museum
The staff of the Public Library, Ashford, Kent
The staff of the Public Library, Folkestone, Kent
Mr John Davies, late of The Camera Shop, Hythe, Kent, for his expertise and
     professionalism

I am indebted to the Governors of Harrow School for permission to reproduce Elizabeth Farren's letter to R.B. Sheridan on page 164. To the Royal Academy of Arts Library for the Lawrence Letters from Elizabeth Farren and to the Hull University Archivist for extracts from the Hotham Papers, (deposited in the Brynmor Jones

Library, Hull University). The extracts from the Diaries of Joseph Farington are from the typed copy of the Farington Diaries, the originals of which are in the Royal Library, Windsor Castle.

Outstanding among printed works has been The London Stage, 1660—1800 Part V. Vol.I. Carbondale, Illinois, 1962 which I have consulted constantly and I am deeply indebted to the editor, Charles Beecher Hogan. The late Dr Charles d'Olivier Farran's typescript, *Farrans of Six Continents*, has also been most helpful.

I am grateful to the following publishers and authors for permission to quote extracts from the books named: Basil Blackwell, *Theatre in the Age of Garrick* by Cecil Price; Curtis Brown Ltd, *Emily, Duchess of Leinster* by Brian Fitzgerald; Dr Arnold Hare, *The Georgian Theatre in Wessex*, and *The Theatre Royal Bath: Orchard Street Calendar;* Oxford University Press, *Journals and Letters of Fanny Burney* ed. Joyce Hemlow; *Thraliana* by Hester Lynch Piozzi (formerly Mrs Thrale) ed. Katharine Balderston; *Diary of Sylas Neville*, ed. by B.Cozens-Hardy; *Lady Elizabeth and the Grosvenors* by Gervas Huxley; The Society of Theatre Research, *The Early Manchester Theatre* by J.L. Hodgkinson and Rex Pogson, and Rupert Crewe Ltd, *Haymarket: Theatre of Perfection* by W. MacQueen Pope.

Bibliography

Manuscript unpublished sources:

FARINGTON, Joseph. Diaries of, Prints & Drawings Room, British Museum. M.S.927–975 (Typescript), the originals of which are in the Royal Library, Windsor Castle.

KEMBLE, J.P., Journals of. Department of Manuscripts. M.S.31 972–975. (B.M.)

VOLUME OF PLAYBILLS of Private Theatricals. Reference Library, British Museum, 937.g.96. Charles Burney.

THEATRICAL REGISTER (notebooks and cuttings etc) vols.1777 – 1797. Reference Library 993.b.I. Charles Burney.

THEATRE PLAYBILLS as above c.120.h.I.

HOTHAM PAPERS. Deposited Brynmor Jones Library, University of Hull.

LETTERS of Sir Thomas Lawrence, P.R.A., Library of the Royal Academy of Arts, London.

FARRAN, Dr Charles d'Olivier, *Farrans of Six Continents*. 1692–1950. 1950. (Typescript).

FARRAN letters and notes (including those of Dr Farran above).

BLOXAM letters, notes and cuttings.

Other Sources

Anonymous (Petronius Arbiter) *Memoirs of the Present Countess of Derby*. 1797. Ref.Lib.B.M.614.I.25.

Anonymous (attributed to R.B. Sheridan). *The Testimony of Truth to Exalted Merit*, 841.I.2. (A Refutation of the above. 1797).

Selection of Books Consulted

Adolphus, John. *Memoirs of John Bannister. 1839*

Bellamy, Thomas. *Miscellanies of Prose and Verse, 1795*. The London Theatres 1795.

Bernard, John. *Retrospections of the Stage. 1830*. 2 vols.

Boaden, James. *Memoirs of Elizabeth Inchbald, 1833*

Boaden, James. *Life of Mrs Jordan, 1831*

Boaden, James. *Memoirs of the Life of J.P. Kemble. 1825*

Boaden, James. *Memoirs of Mrs Siddons. 1826*. 2 vols.

Boswell, James. *Private Papers of, from Malahide Castle, Co.Dublin*, Ed. G.Scott and F.Pottle.

Broadbent, J.R. *Annals of the Liverpool Stage. 1908*

Broadbent, J.R. *Historical Society of Lancashire and Cheshire*. Vol LXI 1910

Burney, Fanny. *The Journals and Letters of*. Ed. Joyce Hemlow 1972–1978. Vols. III& IV [see Hemlow]

Campbell, T. *Life of Mrs Siddons, 1834*

Colman, George, the Younger. *Random Records. 1830*

Cumberland, Richard, *Memoirs. 1806*

Delany, Mrs Mary, *Autobiography and Correspondence*. Ed. Lady Llanover 1861

Doran, Dr John, *Knights and their Days. 1856*

Fitzgerald, Brian, *Emily, Duchess of Leinster. 1950*

Fitzgerald, P.H. *The Good Queen Charlotte. 1899*

Froude, J.A. *Thomas Carlyle; the First Forty Years. 1833*

Galt, John. *Lives of the Players. 1831*

Gore, John. *Life and Times of Thomas Creevey* ed. by ??.1933

Gilliland, Thomas. *The Dramatic Mirror. 1804*

Hare, Dr Arnold. *The Georgian Theatre in Wessex 1958. The Theatre Royal, Bath; Orchard Street Calendar 1750–1805. 1977*

Haslewood, Jos. *The Secret History of the Green Room. 1790*

Hemlow, Joyce. *The Journals and Letters of Fanny Burney.* Volume III & IV. 1973. [see Burney]

Hogan, Charles Beecher. Editor, *The London Stage 1660–1800. Part V. 1776–1800. 1968*

Huxley, Gervas. *Lady Elizabeth and the Grosvenors. 1965*

Kelly, Michael. *Reminiscences. 1826*

Lawrence, Dr W.J. *The Connoisseur, Vol. XXIX no.114 Feb 1911*

Lewes, Charles Lee, *Memoirs 1805* 2 vols

Mathews, Charles, *Memoirs,* 4 vols. 1839

Mathews, Mrs Chas.(Anne) *Tea Table Talk 1839; Anecdotes of Actors 1844*

Meister, Henri. *Letters Written during a Residence in England, 1799*

Maxwell, Sir Herbert, *The Creevey Papers, 1903*

Papendiek, Mrs Charlotte. *Court and Private Life in the Time of Queen Charlotte. 1889*

Patmore, P.G. *The Cabinet of Gems. 1837*

Piozzi, Hester Lynch (formerly Thrale) *Thraliana.* ed. Katharine Balderston. 2 vols. 1942

Piozzi, Hester Lynch (formerley Thrale) *The Intimate Letters to Penelope Pennington.* ed. Oswald Knapp. 1913

Roach's *Authentic Memoirs of the Green Rooms 1796*

Stirling, A.M.W. *The Hothams 1918*

Thrupp, G.A. *History of Coaches 1877*

Waldron, F.G. *Candid and Impartial Strictures on the Performances. 1795; A Compendium History of the Stage, 1800*

Walpole, Horace. *Letters of,* ed. Mrs Paget Toynbee, 19 vols 1903–1925

Wilkinson, Tate *The Wandering Patentee, 1795. Memoirs; 1790*

Williams, D.E. *Life & Correspondence of Sir Thomas Lawrence P.R.A. 1831*

Wilson – Mrs Cornwell Baron-Wilson *Memoirs of Miss Harriott Mellon (afterwards Duchess of St Albans)*

Winston, James. *The Theatric Tourist. 1805*

Wrottesley, Lt.Col. the Hon. George, *Life and Correspondence of Field Marshal Sir John Burgoyne 1873*

INDEX (i)

FARREN (FARRAN) See SMITH-STANLEY, Elizabeth.

SMITH-STANLEY, Elizabeth, née FARRAN (adopted FARREN on stage), COUNTESS OF DERBY, 2nd wife of Edward, 12th Earl of Derby. Classified under headings as follows:-

I   Events of Importance in her life
II   Appearance
III   Biographical References
IV   Character and Characteristics
V   Comments on acting and singing
VI   Health

x x x

I EVENTS OF IMPORTANCE

II APPEARANCE

III BIOGRAPHICAL REFERENCES. Chronological Order

IV CHARACTER AND CHARACTERISTICS

THE FARRAN FAMILY

INDEX (ii)